DARWIN
GOD'S AMBASSADOR

DARWIN
GOD'S AMBASSADOR

Man may die but Heaven is eternal

GEORGE DI PALMA

Matador
5 Weir Road
Kibworth Beauchamp
Leicester LE8 0LQ, UK
Tel: (+44) 116 279 2299
Fax: (+44) 116 279 2277
Email: books@troubador.co.uk
Web: www.troubador.co.uk/matador

ISBN 978 1848762 039

Unless otherwise indicated, scripture has been taken from the
Authorised King James Version of the Bible.

British Library Cataloguing in Publication Data.
A catalogue record for this book is available from the British Library.

Typeset in 11pt Palatino by Troubador Publishing Ltd, Leicester, UK

Matador is an imprint of Troubador Publishing Ltd

Printed in Great Britain by the MPG Books Group, Bodmin and King's Lynn

Dedicated to God's chosen people everywhere, whether in their homeland or afar. May God bless and preserve them for the salvation of mankind.

Author's Note

My perception of modern-day evolutionary philosophy is that of a mythical monster from the deep, raising and lowering its ugly head, occasionally threatening but always failing, unable to emerge from the primeval swamp in which it gave birth. Its roar is worse than its bite and the fire from its belly is losing heat. The weakening monster is slowly dying, sinking into the murky depths from whence it came, with desperate helpers vainly trying to rescue it before it is seen no more.

Chapters

Introduction   *xi*

Preface   *xv*

1   Evolution – A Blessing in Disguise   1

2   A Jewel in Space   26

3   Our Troubled Earth   48

4   The Bible has Answers   67

5   Jesus is the Way   82

6   The Return of Our King   99

7   A Life to Die For   115

Introduction

I believe it was Albert Einstein who said: "If you cannot explain things in simple language then you do not know what you are talking about." Many would agree with him. On such a profound subject as personal destiny, it helps to contemplate as you read and so it becomes necessary to impart a degree of simplicity for the benefit of understanding. Placing trivial disputes over interpretation of biblical dogma to one side, this book will assume a fundamental approach to Christian teaching for the benefit of the reader looking for clarity, at the same time emphasising some basic principles of the creation/evolution dispute.

There is no subject which sparks controversy more than religion. There is no topic which arouses such passionate feelings as personal beliefs, and there is nothing which demands answers more than the question of our origins.

Many sceptics convince themselves that we have no satisfactory answers to the argument that arises out of man's quest for spiritual truth and the reason for human dissension. This is why they remain sceptics. To know truth, we need to search from trusted sources, and in our quest for meaningful answers there is no agency more reliable than the most influential and successful book ever written – The Holy Bible. *"Seek and you shall find,"* proclaimed the words of Jesus Christ.

The manner in which we conduct our lives, the paths we

tread, the judgements we make, all play a crucial role in our ultimate position in the Eternity of Time. As our thoughts precede our actions and actions determine results, our thoughts, assisted by free will, must be carefully nurtured and guided in a Godly direction, if we are to gain an insight into our final place in the cosmos.

There are two major belief systems concerning the origins of mankind. One is that of a Divine Creator and the other is the Darwinian Theory of Evolution. Theistic evolutionists believe that both concepts are possible but as this viewpoint is in conflict with the book of Genesis, I find it easy to dismiss. Changing the word of God is a dangerous occupation.

The creation/evolution debate can be of great assistance in clarifying the many difficult questions that permeate our thoughts on the subject of life hereafter. One way to be assured of a correct earthly path is to ascertain by elimination, which of the two doctrines concerning our origins is genuine. This book presents a clear evaluation of some vital pointers concerning our beginnings, our presence in the universe and our eternal destiny, which may help the reader to discern truth from fiction.

It is vital to realise that despite what sections of the media may portray, no proof or worthwhile evidence exists to endorse evolutionary ideology. If scientific proof for evolution was established, Christianity and other religious institutions would flounder and cease to function. Though people may yearn for proof of God, the arguments and viable indications in favour of a Divine Creator are found to be outstanding, if the search is focused in trusted areas.

This book will not probe into confused issues to explain the differences between our two principles of belief. This is not necessary. We have sufficient clear and comprehensible evidence available to make rational judgements on the subject and the facts will be established with practical expression. If your desire for eternal life is strong enough then the rightful path is open before you. This direction will require a recognition and elimination of all misgivings, allowing you to discern real truth with confidence and assurance.

God did not originally create man to die. Why would He? Man was meant to be immortal but Lucifer, the fallen angel, rebelled against God, tempting Adam into sin and plunging the world into decline. Thereafter we are forced to endure the consequences until Christ returns to restore His creation to its former glory as He promised. It is logical to think that God would want to repair the damage caused by Satan, His enemy, and renew man's eternal status in a new creation.

If you wish to ignore the hope of spiritual enlightenment, live your life for the present and who cares about tomorrow, then that is your choice. But have you paused to consider the consequences if you are wrong? You could be throwing away the prospect of eternal life as proclaimed in God's Bible and that would be a monumental price to pay. Eternal life means exactly that, an existence of peace and harmony forever as promised by the living God, two thousand years ago.

To determine truth, an open style of thinking is required in order for each individual to decide what makes sense and what does not, what is feasible and what is not.

Everyone is aware of the inevitable day that we must part company with Planet Earth. Many of us prefer to brush the idea aside or to totally ignore it. That is not a wise decision: *"Remember man that thou art dust and unto dust thou shall return."* Genesis (3:19). If we knew with some assurance that dying was indeed the last act of our existence, then the issue of death could be abandoned, liberating us to exude life as we please.

Fortunately for humankind, we possess a naturally gifted inclination to contemplate the possibility of a hereafter. Many sceptics too, in their heart of hearts, tend to harbour a thought that beyond this life there could be a new consciousness. My hope in writing this book is to nurture that thought.

There is nothing wrong with having doubts about your faith and this is why true faith is admirable. Christ told us implicitly that perseverance in faith is the golden chalice of our salvation. If your beliefs hover within the uncertainty of agnosticism, the following chapters could help to remove your doubts and guide you into the knowledge and acceptance of your Redeemer, Jesus Christ.

The outcome of your opinions and decisions after reading this book may open the way for a new earthly course but, more importantly, determine your eternal fate. Always remember: God is good news – Evolution is the ultimate bad news.

Preface

In my study of the personality of Charles Darwin and the controversies surrounding this larger than life character, I soon realised that modern neo-Darwinian philosophy was far removed from what the great man had advocated 150 years ago. In reading his work on *The Origin of Species*, I was quite amazed to find the book littered with vague and inconclusive terminology, a Darwinian trait which I later found to be the norm.

Darwin wrote his theory on origins while embarking on a fantasy journey, a fantasy that he wanted to believe and tried to believe, but could not bring himself to believe. He made it clear that confirmation for his theory ultimately rested on transitional fossil findings, yet his theory and the fossil record were poles apart and he knew it. Afraid to publish his manuscript on *The Origin of Species*, it gathered dust for 20 years while he sought answers and verification to the many questions that his theory demanded. Year by year his embarrassment grew at the thought of his bizarre and self-confessed flawed ideology being made known to the outside world.

One day, as I pondered Darwin's projection on transitional fossils (the very essence of his theory), a revelation came to mind. I knew that the absence of transitional or intermediary fossil links was a huge stumbling block, an immovable thorn in the side of Darwinian philosophy and modern-day evolutionism, but a new awareness now permeated my thoughts. I became aware of the fact that there was no requirement for anyone to nullify the theory of evolution. Darwin had disproved his own theory from the grave.

A second revelation soon followed. By the passing of 150 years and the permanent lack of Darwinian criteria (no transitional fossil chains), I realised that the eminent man had unknowingly opened the door to the acceptance of a Divine Creator, a conception that he had contemplated throughout his lifetime. I became convinced that if Darwin was alive today he would readily renounce his theoretic views on origins and gladly place his trust in the assurance of a Divine Creator.

This book was not written to downgrade Darwin's authority or reputation but to enhance it and draw out its true status. Modern-day evolutionists owe Darwin a huge apology for the flagrant disregard and misrepresentation of his principles on origins.

For 150 years, the delusive evolutionary bandwagon has enjoyed a long and easy ride, drawing mankind down a mythical and dangerous path. Our 21st century world needs to see Mr. Darwin in a new light and elevate the man to a position revealing scriptural truth. Pictures of Mr. Darwin displayed alongside the ape are no longer tenable and I find it surprising how little is understood of the inner mind of this man of history. Much of the world at large is still unaware that:

1. Darwin was embarrassed about his evolutionary ideology.
2. Darwin did not conclusively believe in his theory.
3. Darwin harboured great doubts about it.
4. He knew that there was no proof or evidence to endorse it.
5. He knew that his theory was badly flawed.
6. He called it a "Rag of a hypothesis."
7. He strongly insinuated that within a reasonable time period after his death, certainly no more than a century, if the criteria

for an evolutionary process was not fulfilled, then his theory must bite the dust.

I believe that some knowledge of creational apologetics, covering the fundamentals of a created universe, would have satisfied the Darwinian intellect that the Creationist or Intelligent Design argument carried much more credibility than the theory on origins which so haunted him. Like many of the evolutionary scientists who have converted to creationism, I feel sure that Darwin would have changed course, having balanced creational facts (unknown in his day) against his speculation on origins.

Evolution cannot explain how the first living cell formulated itself, from non-living matter, as the building blocks of all life forms, plant, animal and human, have to be codified to a precise formula. Any honest evolutionist will admit that lack of transitional fossil evidence is their worst headache, as the fossil record shows that all creatures have never changed identity, demonstrating that a fish was always a fish, a monkey was always a monkey and a human being was always as complete as he is.

From a narrow perspective, some evidence for evolution may seem persuasive until you learn about the evidence for creation. Then the evidence for evolution becomes incongruous.

Like his fellow genius Einstein, Sir Isaac Newton emphasised the significance of simplicity in explaining complex issues: *"Truth is ever found in simplicity, and not in the multiplicity and confusion of things."* I have endeavoured to comply with this rule throughout the following chapters, for the benefit of those searching for simple answers. Sir Isaac also stressed the logical conclusion to be drawn from the perceptions around us: *"When I look at the solar system, I see the earth at the right distance from the sun to receive the proper amounts of heat and light. This did not happen by chance."*

Though evolutionary dogma is a small minority world

view, the concept has caused great damage to communal and Christian values for over a century, resulting in world mayhem, both socially and politically.

In Darwin's time and to this day, the primary reason for the acceptance of an evolutionary point of view is that it presents to the follower an excuse not to believe in God. The consequences of this opinion are clearly apparent throughout our troubled world.

CHAPTER ONE

Evolution – A Blessing in Disguise

Before the concept of evolution began to violate the minds of men around 150 years ago, the majority of people believed in some type of deity, while the minority were unsure of their spiritual convictions. Unexpectedly, a strange theory about the origin of life was released to the world and people at the time who were reluctant to believe in God, clutched onto the idea like a vice, not pausing to consider whether this mystifying ideology might be true or unfounded. Since that time, ungodly people (not necessarily wicked people) have manipulated, distorted and expanded this theoretic notion, in the attempt to justify their own ungodliness. For the past century and a half, in the trail of the theory, Evolutionism and Christianity have been locked in battle over their conflicting doctrines.

In recent times, a worldwide debate has raged between Creationists and Evolutionists, almost emerging into war. There is certainly a war of words going on, with the debate reaching new levels of complexity, as one side counter-argues with the other. Creationists are repeatedly taking the debate to new heights of understanding, giving us a clear evaluation of our origins, our purpose on this earth and our final destiny. Evolutionary dogma fails to provide us with valid explanations in these areas.

The good news for those torn between the two belief systems is the fact that many highly qualified evolutionists have changed sides and converted to the creationist viewpoint. Many of these scientists and other intellectuals from various fields, thoroughly expert on evolutionary issues, have clearly seen flaws in their previous philosophy and have decided emphatically that the weight of evidence is overwhelmingly in favour of an Intelligent Designer being responsible for the creation of our universe, the solar system and life on earth.

These learned men have had the integrity to abandon their faulty evolutionary views and now gladly embrace the principles of creation. When men of conviction have worked as experts on opposing sides of an argument, they are worthy of attention. Though there may be one or two, for reasons of apostasy, I know of no creationist who has converted to an evolutionary standing.

Darwin the Romanticist

Many people casually believe that Charles Darwin proved his theory of evolution. Is this true? Before deciding, it is imperative that we take a closer look at the character of this famous man. History tells us that Mr. Darwin was a tall-story teller and he liked nothing more than to shock his contemporaries with barbarous tales of the unorthodox. Darwin did not inaugurate the concept of evolution but was the first to promulgate the idea. I believe it was his grandfather who aspired to promote the notion of evolutionary development, and consequently it became the ambition of his grandson Charles to popularise the wishes of his grandfather. Spurred on by this ambition he wrote his book *The Origin of Species* attempting to disclose how man emerged from primitive life form, through various biological intermediaries, to his present status.

However, having completed his manuscript, Darwin was faced with an insurmountable problem. He had reflected deeply on the criteria by which evolutionary concepts would need to be proven, but to his dismay, the criteria which could only be found in the fossil record did not exist.

Darwin's Dilemma

For the Theory of Evolution to be proven, the fossil record must show transitional fossil formations demonstrating the change from one species into another. In reality, the theory demands that there be: *"Numerous transitional or intermediate forms of fossils at every level of strata"* – the words of Charles Darwin. He was clearly indicating that fossil-finds at that time were not supporting his theory as they must. This left him perplexed and frustrated. He went on to say: *"Why then is not every geological formation and every stratum full of such transitional links? Geology assuredly does not reveal any such finely graduated chain, and this perhaps is the most obvious and serious objection which can be urged against the theory."* In simple terms, he was stating that his theory lacked verifiable facts.

The complexity of the eye posed a particular dilemma for Darwin. He had this to say: *"To suppose that the eye with all its inimitable contrivances for adjusting the focus to different distances, for admitting different amounts of light and for the correction of spherical and chromatic aberration, could have been formed by natural selection, seems I freely confess, absurd to the highest degree."* Darwin was principled enough to admit that his theory of evolution posed many questions and was far from proven.

While Darwin made outstanding contributions to biological science, he made one huge error concerning his evolutionary speculations. He failed to differentiate macro-evolution from micro-evolution, the latter showing a variation within the species. Variation produces many kinds of cats but they are still cats. There are many kinds of dogs but they remain dogs and there are many types of monkeys but they still belong to the monkey species. This variation is peculiar to all forms of living things, including man, but the micro-evolutionary process can never produce new or separate species. Either Darwin failed to make the distinction clear or modern day evolutionists have incorporated the two systems to suit their projections. I suspect both.

Darwin's intention in advocating the theory of macro-evolution (the change of one species into another) was to hand it over for scientists to prove. 150 years later, scientists have been unable to produce one piece of viable evidence to support any macro-evolutionary development. Unfortunately for subsequent generations, and to this day, anti-God evolutionists have chosen to dismiss this failure. They also refuse to question the fact that Darwin, having transcribed his theory, was hesitant in having it published, and deliberated for twenty years on whether to disclose his strange thesis to the outside world. If he was assured and confident about the truth of his proposals, one would have expected Darwin to be eager in presenting his book for public scrutiny. Not so. His embarrassment concerning the lack of evidence for his theory was deep rooted. There were no transitional fossil chains to endorse the project, so his manuscript lay dormant, causing the great man insufferable torment. Being of proud mind and unable to concede defeat, Darwin stubbornly persisted with his speculations, but having deceived himself and being master of argumentation, he was adept in convincing others that his unfounded theory was genuine.

Darwin was a churchgoer and Bible reader, which left him with a burden of guilt concerning his thoughts on origins, and he frequently wrestled with his conscience about the possible existence of God, and never came to terms with his dilemma. The great man, in his quest for evidential truth, became torn between God and his theory.

Darwin the Sceptic

What were the thoughts of Charles Darwin concerning Godly beliefs? Many people of today routinely believe that Darwin was an atheist, but history tells us that Darwin pondered deeply on the possibility of a Creator. He openly expressed his views: *"I have never been an atheist in the sense of denying the existence of God. Agnostic would be a more correct description of my state of mind."* At this point, may I remind the steadfast evolutionary brigade of Darwin's true convictions on the divinity: *"The mystery of the beginning of things is insoluble, and I for one must be content to remain agnostic."* These words by the eminent man show that he was never anti-God, but they do confirm why he was embarrassed by his evolutionary visions. Maybe this explains a reluctance to reveal his dubious theory to the outside world? As Darwin proclaimed himself agnostic, this seriously diminishes his belief in his own theory.

Darwin suffered from ill-health for most of his life. Being a deep thinker, he was also prone to high stress levels and frequently doubted the truth of his representation of our origins. On the declaration of his theory, he privately admitted to his peers: *"It is a mere rag of a hypothesis with as many flaws and holes as sound parts."*

Neo-Darwinian enthusiasts prefer to ignore these facts of history. If they could bring themselves to accept the statements of Darwin as written and view the Bible as written, they would, I am sure, be better placed to make sound evaluations.

Darwin's theory, by self-admission, was open-ended. His challenge to palaeontologists was for them to unearth the necessary criteria to underpin his hypothesis. In essence, he was pointing out that future subterranean fossilised discoveries must fulfil the criteria attached to his theory, otherwise mankind must be humble enough to bow down to a Universal Creator.

Darwin's Decline

After his young daughter Annie died, and blaming God for the loss, Darwin never attended church again and the ambition of his evolutionary objectives took on a vengeful expression. When Mr. Alfred Wallace was about to publish a similar book on origins, the proud Darwin in panic mode could not restrain himself, and he decided to impose his curious and questionable theory of evolution onto the human race. Whether his theory was valid or not, he could not be beaten by his contemporary.

In a morose state of mind, he decided to publish his book *The Origin of Species* knowing unequivocally that the publicity engendered would embarrass the Christian church and cause havoc with biblical teachings. Around the same period, his colleague Charles Lyell, an eminent geologist, also had a problem with Christianity. Having lapsed from his faith, he systematically attempted to discredit the teachings of Moses - his intention being that if the doctrines of Moses, author of the foundational book of Genesis, could be disproved then Christianity would inevitably disintegrate. Fortunately for mankind, his venture failed and in retaliation, although he disagreed with the evolutionary concept, Lyell was eager to endorse the theory and encouraged Darwin in spreading his unconfirmed ideology of the origin of man.

There we have the source and foundation of Darwinian hypotheses. Nothing was discovered and nothing was proven. The Theory of Evolution enfolded largely as a deception, born out of animosity towards God and the Christian faith. Now, at the outset of the 21st century, the original and fictitious evolutionary imposition has escalated to outlandish proportions.

No Time Left

Darwin lived in hope that the passage of time might eventually reveal sufficient lines of transitional fossil forms to cement his theory. To date, not one transitional fossil link has been found and established. Not one continuous fossil chain showing the transition of one species into another exists today and man has never witnessed any species of life changing into another. All of the so called transitional fossils on display in museums are micro-evolutionary linked, rendering to the observer a false impression. 150 years ago the fossil record was poor, but that cannot be said today. There are over 100 million fossils displayed in museums around the world at this present time without the presence of one viable intermediary fossil of macro-evolutionary extraction. Each time a supposed skeletal link between ape and man is found, the bones in question always turn out to be either totally ape or completely man. Some evolutionists freely admit that the fossil record is not compatible with evolutionary development, casting further suspicion on any credibility for the theory.

One must conclude from evidence of the fossil record which is now considerably advanced, that transitional fossil formations have never existed or they would have been unearthed without too much difficulty. If, by evolutionary presumption, life on earth had begun to emerge over two billion years ago with the ensuing deaths of many trillions of life forms, one would expect the earth to be saturated with, as Darwin stated, numerous intermediary fossil links. Fossils of the various forms of life which have been unearthed the world over continually show creatures to have been fully formed with no gradualism. This is what we would expect to find if life was created in the beginning, as decreed in the book of Genesis. The fossil record and biblical doctrine are totally compatible.

Darwin suspected that within the confines of a century after his time, the fossil issue should resolve itself one way or the other, liberating the world from a quandary of doubt. He surmised that knowledge of our origins either from primitive descent or ingenious creation would sound the death knell of agnosticism. Now, in the 150th anniversary of his famous and infamous work, with fossil findings conclusively in favour of creation, the renowned gentleman has condemned his theory from the grave. What evolutionists choose to ignore is that a theory remains a theory until proven.

The Big Fallacy

Some evolutionary concepts are difficult to evaluate. All scientists agree that the universe had a beginning and prior to that beginning there was nothing. The initiation of the birth of the universe, according to evolutionary dogma, exceeds human comprehension. Evolutionary education is instructed to accept what we know to be impossible – scientifically impossible. We are directed to believe that nothing exploded. This surely is the most bizarre statement of all time. The big bang was supposedly so big that it is still expanding and therefore still destructive, allegedly after 13 billion years, and all from nothing. This brash and speculative account of the origin of the universe is the initial reason why Creationists confidently advocate the deception of a billion age universe. I have mentioned the first phase in this deception but there are many more.

Let us concentrate on this assumed explosion for a while. We know that the one and only result from an explosion is chaos and the bigger the explosion the bigger the chaos. One would logically deduce that the disorder produced by an explosion which is still in progress and therefore continually destructive after 13 billion years could not possibly produce order. This is basic science.

In contrast, let us consider the condition of our earth and solar system. Our earth, sun, moon and planets move in conjunction with one another in complete harmony. We know that the solar system rotates in synchronised order, but we also know that chaos and order cannot exist simultaneously, as only one state or the other can be maintained. Therefore scientifically, either the solar system or the big bang theory is in error. But man has known for a long time that the solar system is a reality and is in perfect order, therefore it is elementary to conclude that the assumed big bang theory is a grave misconception. Creationist scientists can adequately demonstrate how the big bang theory suggests the impossible, as it contradicts the natural laws of physics. Evolutionary scientists also know this but are willing to accept the anomaly. The big bang concept is no more than an unproven assumption.

We know without question that the first two concepts of

evolution are scientific impossibilities. Nothing comes from nothing and an explosion cannot transform itself into an organised system. Let me form a correlation to the solar system suggestively emerging out of a big bang. Take the case of a clock factory with thousands of spare parts waiting to be assembled into clocks. Suddenly there is an enormous explosion and all of the spare parts are blown skywards. If you are to believe the big bang theory then you must believe that some of those spare parts could somehow assemble themselves into perfectly made clocks, working in unison. If you are an evolutionist then you must concede to the possibility of such an absurdity.

Foundations of any belief system are of paramount importance. If those foundations are based on falsification and scientific impossibilities then the remainder of the concept becomes incongruent. Despite that, the indoctrination of evolutionary ideology abounds. The evolutional account of the birth of our universe bears no adherence to scientific principle. A more acceptable explanation for the beginning of things can be found in the Good Book, Genesis 1:1. There we have a detailed and chronological order of our initial creation which falls in line with scientific analysis.

The line of assumed evolutionary progression is bewildering. From nothing to an explosion of infinite proportions, early life supposedly and mysteriously emerged from particles, atoms and molecules, which magically turned into lakes of primeval soup. This sequence ostensibly happened by chance, and that is only the beginning. After great leaps of millions of years, it is claimed, the soup ingeniously turned into fish meandering around in vast oceans, and to this day the evolutionists have no valid explanation for where the prodigious amounts of sea water on our planet came from.

In line with evolutionary extrapolation, the fish then

acquired the inclination to walk and live on land. It would take millions of years, of course, and they would have to grow legs and completely change their body structure and perhaps convey their intentions onto subsequent generations. At this point, I think you will agree that the last place a fish would want to live is out of water. This apart, the evolutionists are telling us to believe in this magical transformation. They scornfully mock the supernatural powers of a Divine Creator, while adopting unnatural concepts for their own creeds.

The fish, now amphibians, wish to move on. Having lived on land for millions of years, they decide to convert. Why not change into reptiles? And they do, just like that. Well, it will take millions of years, but no matter, they will get there. The reptiles, totally ignorant of the laws of aviation, then decide to sprout wings and fly, and why not? After yet another span of millions of years these reptiles are now birds flying above the earth, but wait, they have changed their minds again. After a further stretch of millions of years they wish to discard their wings and come down to earth once more. If you were a bird, do you think you would want to lose your wings? Over millions of years they get rid of their wings and turn into mammals, but they have not finished yet.

The evolutionists tell us quite unashamedly that a strain of the mammal population turned into apes and now, hey presto, the hominid genus is Homo sapiens. Yes, the human race has arrived in all its glory, the finished article. Or is it?

Are You Changing?

At this stage of the peculiar odyssey, there is an enormous split in evolutionary dogma. Many evolutionists believe that we stopped evolving 100,000 years ago, while others say we are not the finished article. The foundational meaning of evolution is continual change therefore to be a true evolutionist you are compelled to believe that we are in a continual state of altering our physique and are changing into some other, as yet unknown creature, completely different from our present shape or form. Do you detect any signs of evolutionary change in your make-up? Do you wish to shake off your human form and evolve into a different type of creature? According to the evolutionists, fish and reptiles accomplished the feat, then birds and monkeys followed, so why can't we?

Here is one more problem for the evolutionist. We are decidedly of higher intellect than fish, reptiles, birds and monkeys and our intelligence tells us that we could not possibly will ourselves to change limbs and body organs or grow wings to fly, so how could exceedingly lesser intelligent creatures have done so? The evolutionary concept that creatures either willed themselves to change or the changes occurred of their own volition defies logic, scientific assessment and biogenetic science. These presumed modifications have never been observed and each step of the supposed evolutionary process is engulfed in loose, speculative, wild assumptions, contrary to all known biological data.

Despite the multitude of anomalies that the evolutionists have to face, they stubbornly adhere to the view that the development of life was self-instigated, a process which is unexplainable. Body organs need to be complete in order to carry out their function, for example the eye, heart and brain. This would be impossible with super slow gradual changes over millions of years. It is not difficult to understand that a partially formed reproduction system could not work. As the reproductive mechanisms of biological life systems vary enormously in size, shape and function, it is impossible to evaluate how one kind could restyle itself over millions of years and maintain the process of biogenetic science.

There are many practical examples which negate evolutionary origins and point us in the direction of biogenesis. World population growth is a prime example, as you will read in the next chapter. If man arrived at his present status around one million years ago as the evolutionists claim, then where is the trail of history? Written history began around the time of Abraham 4,000 years ago. Before that time, apart from the biblical account, we have no record of any kind of life. If intelligent man had been roaming the earth for a million years, his indelible mark would have scarred the earth to such an extent that undeniable proof of his ancestry would abound. His fossilised footprints, fingerprints and etchings would far outstrip the petty few controversial discoveries claimed by evolutionary palaeontologists. Compared to the progress which man has achieved over the last century, the advancement he could potentially have accomplished over a million year period would be clearly astronomical, with the car, plane and computer arriving many thousands of years ago. The logical reason why we have a totally blank record of a million years of man's historical presence is because earth and man have existed for only a fraction of that time-span, vis-à-vis the 6,000 years of creational history.

Since the Darwinian era, great advances have been made in the scientific and biological fields of discovery. Scientists have determined that our DNA could not possibly have evolved. DNA is present in its entirety and scientific knowledge can now present us with clearly defined biological information to demonstrate how it eliminates any evolving process.

For a long time it was believed that the spark of

evolutionary progression was instigated by changes or mistakes in the genes (mutations). Natural selection presumes that mutations are beneficial and it was previously assumed that mutational modification resulted in added information, thus enabling the process of evolution to advance. This has been the so called biological proof of macro-evolution over the decades. Modern scientific technology shows that mutations are decisively harmful as they damage the information in the DNA, resulting in less information. This mutational change precipitates a backward step, making any evolutionary process biologically impossible. The evolutionist, Pierre-Paul Grasse clearly stated: *"No matter how numerous they may be, mutations do not produce any kind of evolution."* Modern knowledge of DNA and mutational reaction was denied to 19th century scientists. Some degree of perception by Darwin of these biological principles would have killed his theory stone dead and he could not have written his book *The Origin of Species.*

Being a Bible reader, Darwin could have been aware of the link between our fallen world and the concept of the survival of the fittest (natural selection). Docile and vegetarian eating animals became wild and ferocious after the fall of man, as proclaimed in the book of Genesis, when all creatures were thereafter plunged into a world of survival. The concept of natural selection, an idea stolen by Darwin from a colleague, bears no correlation to evolution and is testimony to Darwin's expertise in expressing vagueness in his writings on origins. A better understanding of Genesis would have debunked Darwin's natural selection thesis and spared him years of deliberation concerning his theoretic speculations. It is ironic that Darwin could have found answers to many of his intellectual predicaments in the Good Book adorning the shelves of his own study. This single oversight has resulted in the degrading of human elevation for the past 150 years.

Many contemporary scientists are moving away from Darwinism, and the acceptance of an Intelligent Designer being responsible for the construction of our universe is rapidly gaining ground. Most scientists have given up trying to produce life from non-life. If life emerged by itself in the beginning from nothing, then one would feel that modern-day scientists could be capable of reproducing it. Having undergone countless experiments over the years, using all the state of the art technology available, scientists have repeatedly failed in their endeavour to produce life systems from inert matter, and if they did, it would prove that it took intelligence to do it. Those who vehemently use the intelligence which their Creator has bestowed on them, to try and disprove that He created them are affording God the greatest of insults.

In the attempt to discern truth from fiction on the origins issue, it helps to move away from complex analysis and apply some natural logic. A bicycle cannot change into a car and then a house. This fundamental principle applies to individual species of living things, which have never been known to change their classification. A mouse cannot change into a dog and then a horse, and a fish cannot change into a reptile then a bird. Also, there is zero evidence to suggest that a monkey could ever change into a human being, as the evolutionists fatuously believe. The fossil record demonstrates that these changes have never occurred and placing one's trust in such metaphysical alteration requires a mountain of faith.

Frauds and Hoaxes

Evolutionists have been so frustrated by repeated failures to substantiate their beliefs that many of them have resorted to the perpetration of frauds and hoaxes spanning the last 100 years. Piltdown man, Nebraska man and Java man are prime examples of cleverly orchestrated frauds which were eventually exposed, and there have been a host of others. The creationists are forced to be constantly on the alert to uncover any attempts to fabricate lies as truth, which deprive the world of the knowledge of their Creator.

Most people are familiar with tales of Neanderthal man portrayed as backward, uncivilized and ape-like. There is now strong evidence to the contrary and many experts believe that Neanderthal was as human and intelligent as we are. Tests have shown that he walked with a stoop because he suffered from rickets and severe arthritis. Nobody knows what he truly looked like as he has never been excavated intact. Characterisations of him with ape-like features based on guesswork and imagination are the work of diehard evolutionists vainly attempting to establish a link between ape, Neanderthal and man.

Why do evolutionary fanatics continue with this fraudulent war against the creationists? The reason is that they do not want to believe in God. They are opposed to being subservient to a Divine authority and refuse to humble themselves. They want to be free to live as they please, with no moral or ethical guidelines. The Bible has clearly defined their position in warning them that if they move away from God, He will move away from them. The book of Timothy foretold of the evolutionary delusion and the reluctance of man to accept truth: *"And they shall turn away their ears from the truth, and shall be turned into fables"* (11 Timothy 4:4). The evolutionary myth is the most notorious of these fables.

The most infamous fraud was perpetrated by Ernst Haeckel, a German biologist and evolutionist, towards the end of the 19th century. Haeckel deliberately made fake drawings of human embryos with gill slits, to give the impression that man evolved from fish. He published his fraudulent drawings in 1868 to deceive the world into believing the evolutionary lie. Though his cunning trick was uncovered by a chemist in 1875, he dared to write a book *Natural History of Creation* in 1883, which illustrated his forgeries. Later, he was brought to trial and convicted. Some years before his death in 1909, he confessed to his outrageous behaviour, but to this day his book remains in circulation throughout the world. This scandal of the highest proportion continues to entice many of our children into believing the fabrication of our origins, drawing them away from Christian values.

If evolution was fact, with good evidence for support, there would be no necessity for the continued perpetration of fraudulent manipulation. These deceptions are testimony to the lack of evidence which evolutionists are searching for in vain. Evolutionary mania, which began as a wild and unrestrained idea, has emerged as a virtual religious institution. With poor evidence for support, stubborn followers of Darwin have forced themselves and others to rely purely on faith, 100 percent blind faith. Conversely, the creationists while also depending on a modicum of faith to accompany a wealth of biological, cosmological and naturalistic evidence, can be confident that their faith is certainly not blind. It is a reflection of our fractured world, as expressed in chapter three of this book, that such a blatantly misguided concept as evolution could gain such a stranglehold over its followers, with the potentially damaging effect on their eternal salvation.

Why is it that some evolutionary geologists date fossils by the age of the rocks in which they are found, while others date rocks by the age of the fossils found in those rocks? Their findings are then placed in the assumed millions of years category, without any foundation for their epic time-scales. Geologists on behalf of creation can adequately explain the entire geological formation of the earth, covering a period of a few thousand years, in line with the biblical account of Genesis and the aftermath of the worldwide flood.

As the creation/evolution debate deepens, evolutionists are becoming increasingly frustrated as they continue to fail in their attempts at finding good evidence in favour of evolutionary development. Professor Richard Dawkins, science's leading evolutionary biologist has freely admitted: *"I believe but I cannot prove that all life, all intelligence, all design and all creativity in the universe is the direct or indirect product of Darwinian natural selection."* If a morsel of genuine evidence for evolution existed, he would not have made that statement. Darwin's book on origins contains a conglomerate of suppositions, with a continuous stream of words like maybe, could, and if. Suggestion is frequently used, with such phrases as possibly been, seems to be, and may perhaps. Neo-Darwinism has converted this vagueness into the false concept of certainty.

The Big Delusion

The structure of contemporary evolutionary education is enshrouded in guesswork, speculation and unproven assumptions. This is fantasy-land portrayed as factual-land. Evolutionary instruction cannot define the theoretic process in lucid and comprehensible language. The wisdom of Einstein, as stated in the initial words of the introduction to this book, demands that they should and exposes their convoluted interpretations. Mr. Darwin would not take kindly to the latter-day falsification and countless misrepresentations of his renowned theory. The evolutionary account of our origins was formulated by a brilliant but tormented mind, which failed to discern fact from fiction, and now presents its supporters with a host of unanswerable questions.

Darwinism Abused

Those of questionable motives are continually attempting to keep the speculation of evolution alive to suit their own worldly interests and are willing to ignore the massive amounts of evidence for creation around them. Others live under the delusion that evolution is confirmed truth, oblivious of the evidence for or against it.

The belief that we could magically emerge from nothing, that life came from non-life and that cultured human beings ascended from pools of viscous slime, exceeds human perception. Some evolutionists admit to the absence of any progressive fossil chain which links fish, reptiles, birds, mammals and humans and this is the pivotal argument of the entire debate. Darwin was adamant on this point. He was stating emphatically that:

Transitional fossil chains prove his theory.
Non existence of them, abolishes his theory.

From a Darwinian viewpoint, this is the nucleus of his ideology, the heart of the philosophy, and all other evolutionary issues concerning man's origin are secondary. The sceptics of this world must be given the opportunity to ascertain that this impulsive and outlandish idea on origins, albeit of astute and imaginative intellect is contrary to natural and scientific law, and is having the effect of drawing them away from their divinely ordained eternal path.

It must be significant that some scientists have exhausted their life's work trying to authenticate the theory of evolution and have totally failed. The truth is that the theory does not present us with a feasible account to which we can relate, and sadly, generation after generation continues to be hoodwinked into believing the evolutionary lie. Many people willingly follow an ungodly evolutionary direction because it merges with their comfort zone. It breaks them free of any moral or divine authority, allowing them to go their own way, thus appointing themselves as their own master.

If evolution was an established fact, the global media would be inundated with the evidence at hand, leaving us in no doubt about its validity. The proof of evolution would be the collapse of Christianity, as people ceased to worship. Churches, synagogues and mosques would close and the clergy would disappear. Atheists and evolutionists would turn our cathedrals into museums to show the world that they had buried God forever. But what would happen next? Worldwide anarchy would abound. We would experience the disintegration of law and order, with societies as we know them degenerating into mayhem. Fortunately, that will never happen. Christian values and Godly ways are the standards that hold society together. Our evolutionary friends like to point out that churches are half empty but I see them as half full. In many countries they are full and overflowing.

Out of six billion people in the world, over 30 percent belong to Christian denominations. Around 15 percent are Muslims who also refute evolution, and approximately 15 percent belong to other religious groups. Around 30 percent of the world's population are estimated to be of uncertain agnostic persuasion, leaving a minority of less than 10 percent who adhere, in some capacity, to evolutionary beliefs. The steadfast evolutionists must, in my opinion, number no more than a few million, but sadly, it is those few million, and in particular those with media influence, who are shouting the loudest and peddling the false doctrine of man's ancestry.

If man's evolution was valid, museums around the world would be crammed with millions of consecutive lines of transitional fossil links, encompassing most creatures known to man, including man. The supposed two billion years of biological history should provide us with a clearly defined path of the progression. This would be the only Darwinian directed way to prove that man evolved on this earth.

Unwilling to accept sound creational evidence, evolutionary palaeontologists are frantically scavenging in vain to unearth non-existent intermediary fossil pieces. In order to cover up their failures, some of these scientists are using the argument that transitional fossils are too small to find. The fact is, the earth beneath our feet can either present us with evolutionary validation or nullify it. Time for certification of the former has run out, enabling Christians in doubt and hovering agnostics to move forward with confidence in the knowledge of their Creator. The fossil record corroborates the biblical account of creation.

At this present time, many scientists decisively agree that transitional fossil intermediates do not exist because they have never existed. The criteria laid down by Charles Darwin disproves his own theory beyond doubt, and I am convinced that if Darwin could return to this earth, on discovering the non-existence of any transitional fossil linkage among the 100 million fossils we have unearthed, he would readily admit to his gargantuan mistake. The most fundamental principle of Darwinism has destroyed the theory of evolution and modern scientific knowledge has endorsed that verdict.

150 years after the publication of his thesis, it is not Darwin who is the enemy of God and Christianity, it is the perpetration and perpetuation of 21st century neo-Darwinian propaganda in keeping the mythical evolutionary bandwagon rolling, which is a plague on society. The offshoot of this execution is the proliferation of crime, abortion, drug abuse, world strife and the growth of secular humanism. The final product is the incessant degrading of humanitarian values. Maybe the Darwinian intellect foresaw the aftermath of his written work, when he acclaimed that revealing his theory was like "committing murder." He later referred to his work as "My accursed book."

Humankind is on a higher level than any evolutionary station. With knowledge of the true facts, it is my opinion that the only reason a section of the human race would continue to believe the evolutionary lie, is that in rejecting their Creator, they wish to believe it. One cannot agree with Darwinian philosophy while ignoring the criteria for verification of the hypothesis. The absence of self-asserted criterion proof of evolution by Darwin makes Darwinism implausible.

In its conception, evolution was a fantasy. 150 years later it remains a fantasy and can never be ratified in the eyes of the world. This is the best possible outcome for Christianity. It means that future generations can be confident in a Creator who injected the breath of life into their souls and brought them into the world for the purpose of eternal fulfilment. The tragedy is that the followers of evolution are denying their Maker the glory of His Creation and depriving themselves of the promise of eternal life. This is the ultimate insult to God and His ingenious human conception. There is little doubt that evolutionism has plagued the heart of Christianity throughout the decades and Darwinism has been a hard rock to swallow, but the tide is turning. Maybe, the time has arrived for Christian churches to consider Darwin as a messenger of God. He may well be a friend of God.

The permanent absence of transitional fossil links, by Darwin's admission the Achilles heel of his theory, can galvanise Christian truths. In his flagrant quest for evolutionary notoriety, Mr. Darwin has now, 150 years later, inadvertently revealed the truth of God. The absence of evolution means the presence of a Creator. Darwin was honest about his self-confessed dubious theory. By the passage of time and the complete absence of those infamous intermediary fossil pieces, Darwin has nullified his own theory, opening the door to a deep and heartfelt belief in the one and only alternative – God.

Charles Darwin advocated the possibility of an evolutionary process being responsible for the existence of life on earth, but in the long term has determined the existence of a Creator. They say that God works in mysterious ways. As the world has reeled from the repercussions of this damning theory, could it not be possible that God used Darwin, in a circuitous way, to test the faith of man, to separate the wheat from the chaff and establish His divine purpose in the universe.

I contend that Mr. Charles Darwin is now the contemporary advocate for the existence of a Divine Creator, but blindly, the secular world has not yet tumbled to the fact. The time has come for the world to acknowledge the truth of evolutionary criteria enforced by the eminent man. The time is appropriate for Creationists and Christian denominations to recognise Darwinism as a blessing in disguise which has reached maturity. For the past century and a half, secularists have used Darwinian projection as a bench mark to either ignore or ridicule their Creator, to degrade Christian values and hinder our children's education.

As material evidence for the existence or non-existence of God depends essentially on the results of the criteria affirmed by Darwin (i.e. the existence or non-existence of transitional fossil chains showing man's emergence from inert matter, to animals, to man), then the outcome of that criteria is decisive.

If, by Darwinian assertion, the presence of fossil links were to prove evolution, then the absence of his criteria (no fossil links) must certify the fact of creation.

The implication by Darwin that lack of fossil corroboration did not necessarily invalidate his theory could only have been relevant for his time, as it can no longer be said that fossil links have yet to be discovered. Conclusive fossilized evidence shows that Darwinian criteria has failed to materialise and you will search, in vain, to find a single fossil chain demonstrating the transformation of any species of life into another.

From geological evidence, the absence of water lines indicate the lack of water and the non-appearance of fossil cinders imply the exclusion of fire, therefore no transitional fossil links signify no evolution. The non-existence of transitional fossil chains out of the 100 million fossils uncovered by palaeontologists proves there was never any such process as evolution. Knowing Darwin's obsession for substantiated truth, not forthcoming in his day, I am certain that the illustrious man, in possession of a crystal ball, would have been in complete agreement with this ultimate resolve.

This establishes Mr. Charles Darwin as our leading exponent for the evidential and non-spiritual confirmation of the existence of a Divine Creator. For many decades Darwin was a champion for evolution. Today he is a champion of God.

CHAPTER TWO

A Jewel in Space

On his journey to the moon, the American astronaut Neil Armstrong peered through the window of his space rocket and witnessed the most magnificent sight seen by man. He was looking at God's creation through God's eyes – a blue and radiant jewel in the sky, the home of mankind. As he gazed at this bewitching sight and overcome by the wonder in front of him, there was only one statement that could have emerged from his lips, "Yes," he proclaimed, "there really is a God."

Other astronauts with the same experience, on returning to earth, have undergone a deep and lasting change in their lives. Perhaps, if the sceptics of this world could encounter God's creation from a similar viewing point, they might encounter a similar kind of spiritual enlightenment. Regardless of various religious standpoints, there is no doubt that our earth occupies a unique place in the cosmos and the inhabitants therein subscribe to a special and meaningful purpose. Knowing that purpose may come easy for some people, but for others it can take a lifetime.

Contemporary man is faced with two belief systems regarding his origin. If he has reason to believe that one of those concepts is false, it makes sense to explore the one alternative. Apart from the biblical account, we cannot categorically prove that creation is true, but we can rest in the assurance that our supposed beginnings from nothing or inert matter is a scientifically impossible observation, as revealed in the previous chapter. With the fallacy of an interminable process of man's emergence laid to rest, the principle that a Divine Intelligence breathed life into our earth and universe, becomes embraceable.

Our inquisitive natures are in need of proof and we can never receive an overabundance of facts and information to satisfy our craving for the meaning of life. Unlike the Darwinian concept, which offers no purpose for our occupation of this planet and leaves us with the depressing notion that we came from nowhere, for no reason and we are going nowhere, we can derive comfort in the truth of a God who loves us enough to have shed His blood in payment for our iniquities.

Having buried all notion that we emerged from the animal kind, an enlightened world becomes available to us, with a new embodiment of self-worth, confidence and hope enriching our souls. The knowledge of God is very comforting and our earthly home (albeit temporarily broken) which He created for us, is a clear indication of His invention and purpose. In the midst of earthly unpleasantness we are surrounded by a naturalistic earthly beauty, not of man, which could only have emerged from a high celestial presence.

John Polkinghorne (20th century British scientist and author) stated his opinion of God's creation: *"The intellectual beauty of the order discovered by science is consistent with the physical world as having behind it the mind of a Divine Creator."* When we are able to find solace in our Maker, the thought of having to leave this world, one day, becomes less daunting. I know of people who are genuinely looking forward to their departure from this earthly domain, to eagerly meet up with the One who has promised total renewal.

Let us explore the evidence which informs mankind that he did not emerge from some murky primeval bog, but was created by a loving and caring Master, whose invention in the beginning was perfect, then was subsequently ruined as it is today, but will be restored to its former glory, perhaps in the not too distant future. Just as an honest builder would not construct a defective house for its occupants, likewise, God would not create an imperfect earthly home for its inhabitants. If the creation of God had a perfect beginning, then it must be destined for a perfect ending.

How can we satisfy our curious mentality that a Divine Creator is responsible for our existence and the world which we inhabit? Placing religion to one side for the moment, let us take a closer look at what we already know about the planet, its diversity of life forms, and what allows the variety of living things to function.

The Divine Architect

Humanity, embraced by nature is perched on a rounded mass of energy and matter, suspended in space by its own forces. This particular body mass is unique in the realms of cosmological space. Within man's distant vision but harmful to the naked eye, there is an awe-inspiring dynamic showpiece, 93 million miles from earth, burning constantly and fiercely within strict parameters, providing all species on earth with the necessary heat and light to develop and prosper. Complementing the system, we have an earth satellite closer to home which influences the movement of our ocean tides, playing a vital role in the essential character and balance of our planet.

All three, earth, sun and moon work in motional harmony,

to produce the ideal conditions so necessary for life to thrive as it has done from the birth of the system of things. The earthly home of mankind is a self-regulating body mass.

If the earth and sun were stationed further apart, all earthly life would freeze to death, in fact, life could not have existed from the beginning. If these two bodies in space were closer, all life on earth would frizzle up, or again, we could not have been here to live as we have done, since the advent of nature. If the sun was a larger mass, we would be unable to tolerate the excessive heat. If the sun had been smaller, expelling less heat, man could not have survived the lower temperatures. An appreciably smaller or larger earth would alter the gravitational pull, i.e. respectively we would either float away or be unable to walk upright. If the temperature of the sun was a shade hotter or colder, then life on earth would be impossible. In order for life systems and the essential character of our planet to sustain a natural function, the earth, sun and moon have to be, in every manner and form, precisely as they are – made to measure.

Where did the earth's magnetic field come from? It protects us from the harmful effects of radiation from the sun, providing us with other essential factors, allowing the earth to perform with optimum efficiency. Our earth is two-thirds covered in water. This is the ideal amount required to sustain the earth's natural life systems, otherwise the whole arrangement of nature would be thrown out of balance. How do we receive this water? How does the world acquire an adequate amount of unsalted water to enable our food and crops to grow and to consummate the needs of animal and man?

The inhabitants of earth gratefully accept an amazing self-controlling system in space spanning a distance of 93 million miles that causes the heat of the sun to draw vapour from the oceans and convert it into clouds, which are consistently suspended and whirled at various heights above the earth's surface. During this process, self-induced chemical changes take place. Winds and air currents from around the globe move these clouds into various but strategic positions so that when the vapour is condensed and the clouds heavy, the purified water is distributed around the earth with, for the most part, astonishing regularity and predictable accuracy. The laws of nature ensure that our earth receives this water in harmless droplets, ensuring the distribution is widespread and efficient. Life systems on earth are fully reliant on the continuity of this hydrologic arrangement, which we all take for granted. Could such a system be self-invented or was it the product of divine ingenuity?

The earth is tilted on its axis at an angle of 23.5 degrees. This tilt determines our seasons. If there was no tilt we would have no seasons. If there was more or less tilt, the seasons would be excessively hot or extremely cold. The precise angle ensures the balance of our climate, which in turn determines the growth of trees, flowers and crops. Could man's natural food source be the result of chance solar manoeuvres or was it tailor-made for our needs and enjoyment?

The earth is travelling in a determined orbit round the sun. A faster or slower rate of speed would move it out of position, as the pace of the earth has to be hyper accurate in order to keep it the right distance from the sun. If the earth was spinning faster or slower, our days and nights would be shorter and longer, respectively, causing extremes of temperature incompatible with human limitations. The earth is spinning on its axis and makes a complete turn every 24 hours. This provides a gradual and alternating night of darkness for one half of the planet, which man needs to enable him to rest and replenish his energies for the following day. While 50 percent of the world's population rests, the other half operates as normal, allowing the global workforce to operate ongoing schedules for the integrated and smooth running of commercial world trade.

The earth's moon plays an important part in the equilibrium of oceanic activity and acts as a necessary cog in the mechanism of solar relationships. If the moon was not in its required position, acting as a magnet, then the earth's ocean tides would not synchronize. Could the earth, sun and moon have meandered through space of their own volition, complete with self-engendered systems, and settled in their particular niches, in prime position, performing coherently like the cogs of a watch? Despite the loose evolutionary speculations put forward for the birth and assembly of our solar system, a more logical perception would be that of an intelligent designer having planned it with a particular purpose in mind. The evolutionary presumptuous version for the origin of the solar system is spectacular but unconvincing, and void of reason.

Earth's atmosphere, which consists of 78 percent nitrogen, 21 percent oxygen and one percent other gases is the exact blend needed for life sustenance. Other proportions would not suffice. The gravity of the earth is maintained at the exact strength necessary for man and other creatures to move freely and perform efficiently. Scientists can demonstrate how gravity works but they are at a loss to explain what it is.

Our automated earth is indeed a miracle of invention as expressed in the words of Sir Isaac Newton (17th century British mathematician and physicist): *"This beautiful system of the sun, planets and comets could only produce from the counsel and dominion of an intelligent and powerful Being."* The composition and movement of our earth, sun and moon are governed by closely determined schedules which, like a timepiece, could only have been assembled by a Superhuman Intelligence, as expressed in the following Psalm (40:5): *"Many, O Lord my God, are thy wonderful works which thou hast done."*

The solar system is a huge clockwork mechanism finely tuned in space and all life, all nature depends on this system working with the greatest possible degree of accuracy. The gases in the air we breathe, the elements in the soil needed to grow food, the constituents in our water, are all perfectly formulated to enable life to flourish. The dwelling place of mankind is far too sophisticated to have materialised without the presence and input of a divine coordinator. The concept that, the order and perfection of the solar system together with earthly life and nature, somehow emerged from an explosion out of nothing, defies all scientific assessment. The laws of nature must have been created by someone.

Never by Chance

I have mentioned but a few of the essentials that need to be present and in place for nature and human kind to function. There are countless more. Evolutionists claim that life and the universe came together by chance, without reason or purpose, from a bang that is still in progress. That notion is comparable to throwing a thousand piece jigsaw puzzle into the air and believing it might land fully completed. In theory it could, but in practise it would always be impossible. Man's intellect should advise him, and science confirms it, that nothing comes from nothing and that our earth, solar system and the universe have all the hallmarks of an intelligent architect. The home of mankind operates within a narrow but necessary range of climatic conditions.

The two belief systems of life's origin are poles apart. We

possess the intelligence and free will to determine truth from fallacy and are at liberty to form our own conclusions, but remember what I have written in the introduction to this book. What is feasible and what makes the most sense? Can a house build itself? Does a car invent itself? Can a design or system plan and assemble itself? Not without intelligence behind it. Everything that is made and assembled into a functioning model requires the input of intelligence, and life-systems cannot be excluded. The origin and complexity of earthly life-forms demand, from inception, the insertion of an infinitely higher intelligence than those life-forms. The entity of the "intelligence" of mankind, by intelligent analysis, must have been inaugurated by a higher previously existing mastermind.

Original thought is at the root and foundation of everything that is invented and manufactured on this planet. Does it not follow that the planet, itself a structure of immense complexity, design, balance, beauty and coordination, must be the result of divine thought, construction and purpose.

Evolutionism is at a complete loss to explain the meaning of time, space and matter. The best explication is a bland idea that "it just happened," an assertion which is contrary to all branches of science.

The Unique You

How often do we pause and consider the marvel of engineering genius that forms the composition of the human body? Take a while to contemplate the structure of your inner and outer physique. Observe how your brain, heart, eyes and hearing are so intricately assembled. Marvel at the function of your lungs. Think about the properties in your blood. How did blood originally specify itself and formulate the numerous properties required for bodily operation? Why are your body and limbs shaped the way they are? Why do you have the ability to smile? Who invented the blueprint for you as a human being? Think of your mind (and I do not mean your brain). You are not a body with a mind attached, you are a mind with a body for company. Your mind is you, the unique personality that you are. What is your purpose in the universe and where is your destiny?

Since the beginning of time there has never been another human being like you. Nobody has your eyes or your smile. Nobody has your voice, your fingerprints or your way of interrelating with others, and no one holds to your individual way of thinking. Physically, you are 99 percent the same as your fellow humans but your essential nature and personality places you in a sphere of inimitability. You are not a robot but a unique and special creation, the highest form of life on earth, and your intelligence should cry out to you: "There must be a reason why I exist."

The essence of your being is encapsulated in Psalm (139:14): *"For I am fearfully and wonderfully made."*

First and foremost, as created human beings, we belong to our Creator who sets the rules, and peace of mind can only be found by submission to his will and purpose.

Nature's Intellect

Let us examine some of the necessities in life that we take for granted. Think about nature's way of producing the enormous array of foods for man and beast. Nutrients in the soil absorb carbon dioxide from the air, heat from the sun, and water from the hydrologic cycle to produce every type of food for the nourishment of life. Worms and insects play their part in keeping the soil in good condition. Could the countless variety of flowers, plants, grasses and trees, each with their own life structure, have come about by chance, or do we see invention and design. Natural foods contain a balance of nutrients which our bodies need to be healthy. Our digestive tracts know exactly how to break up and distribute the intake of vitamins and minerals to satisfy the needs of the body. Man was not the brains behind this system of sustenance nor was it engendered by some mythical consultant from outer space.

There are thousands of books which cover every aspect of nature, biology and the human body. The combined knowledge of these books tell us emphatically: "Nature could not have invented itself."

Nature is magnificent, complex and beautiful. Nature is inspiring and methodical. Nature is too well balanced and far too accomplished, to have assembled itself from nothing, as the science of nature requires the presence of initial information with original formulae for all species of life. In the beginning there must have been an intellect which invented the genetic code for each individual life-form. The genetic code is so highly multifarious and self-administering that the assertion of self-invention is not an option of comprehension.

During every micro-second of every day, there are miracles of nature in the conception and birth of living things. The enfolding of new life is awe inspiring. Evolutionary insight is void of any explanatory medium which accounts for the miracle of birth or how the genders of male and female originated. The Bible confirms the law of biogenesis, that all creatures are to produce after their kind and this is exactly what we observe. The evolutionists find it impossible to define where sex came from, but the Bible is specific:

"And the Lord God caused a deep sleep to fall upon Adam, and he slept, and he took one of his ribs, and closed up the flesh instead thereof. And the rib, which the Lord God had taken from man, made he a woman, and brought her into man. And Adam said; This is now bone of my bones, and flesh of my flesh; She shall be called Woman because she was taken out of Man" (Genesis 2:21-23).

"Go forth and multiply," said God, and from that moment on, sex was to be the driving force of God's creation. Our strongest emotion used in its correct domain is a special gift from our Creator and no evolutionary process could have manufactured such a curiosity. The aesthetics of human evolution struggle to give satisfactory answers as to how our positive and negative emotions were born or how natural instinct was formulated. The acceptable answer is that a supreme intelligence programmed the entire biological *modus operandi*.

Nature's arrangement comprises trillions of intricate life systems, large, small and microscopic, which perform in delicate equilibrium. When, on occasion, the balance of nature is knocked off track, it automatically strives to right itself as though it possessed a rationality of its own.

Our Biological Factory

Every one of the 100 trillion cells in our body is a working factory and immeasurably more intricate than the most sophisticated machine ever constructed by man.

Every individual cell is crammed with specific instructions. Each cell generates its own energy in controlling and distributing chemicals around the body. Our cells are so complex and organised that the information within each one would fill hundreds of volumes of books. Learning about the living cell leaves one gasping in awe at its capabilities, and each is fully contained in a capsule 1/1000 of an inch in size. All human beings begin as a single cell which advances and matures into the most refined quintessence in the universe, able to think, evaluate, create and communicate.

If one needs an example of biological Intelligent Design, then a small study of the molecular cell will undoubtedly suffice. The construction of the cell deems any evolutionary process null and void, as the many thousands of parts that make up the working assemblage need to be in place simultaneously. To say that the cell designed and constructed itself is tantamount to believing that the most sophisticated computer could magic itself into existence, or that a library of books could slowly self-compose every word over periods of millennia. The human body is no ordinary structure but an intricate arrangement that more and more scientists are conceding, could not have conjured itself into existence by self-fabrication.

When you have a moment to yourself, hold your hand in front of you and study it carefully. Turn it, twist your wrist and twiddle your fingers. Marvel at its construction, its flexibility and the multitude of tasks it is capable of performing. Then ask yourself: Who initiated such an ingenious implement? Why five fingers of different lengths which amazingly all touch at the same point when stretched forwards? How could your hand be self-invented, complete with fingernails for protection?

Knowledge of DNA, unknown in Darwin's era, kills the evolutionary theory stone dead. DNA is self-replicating. Every aspect of our bodies, from a single hair to the colour of our eyes, from our body dimensions to the colour of our skin is coded with billions of DNA dots, which emphatically distinguish one human being from another. From our knowledge of the DNA molecule, scientists can ascertain the impossibility of any evolutionary process being able to transform one category of life form into another. If Darwin had knowledge of DNA composition, he could not have written his book on the origin of life. The supposed evolutionary development and the function of DNA are totally incompatible.

Time and Space

The vastness of space encompassing our universe is simply mind blowing and the human intellect cannot readily grasp the dimensions involved. If you could travel at the speed of light (some 186,000 miles per second) and you ventured to travel from one side of our galaxy to the other, then your journey would last over 100,000 years. As scientists estimate that there are around 100 billion galaxies in the universe, it perplexes the mind trying to contemplate the distances involved. Galaxies are not in loose alignment but travel with discernible arrangement in conjunction with their celestial neighbours.

The Bible clearly draws our attention to the wonders of the skies: *"Lift up your eyes on high, and behold who hath created these things, that bringeth out their host by number; he calleth them all by names, by the greatness of his might, for that he is strong in power, not one faileth"* (Isaiah 40:26).

As our Creator is greater than the dimensions of time, space and matter, He is truly an Almighty God, and His universe, being a network of coordination, gives us ample reason to procure our faith in Him. The French philosopher, Voltaire, recognised this perception in the words: *"If a watch proves the existence of a watchmaker, but the universe does not prove the existence of a great architect, then I consent to being called a fool."*

Rocket scientist W. Von Braun formed this conclusion: *"The natural laws of the universe are so precise that we have no difficulty in building a space ship to fly to the moon, and can time the flight with the precision of a fraction of a second. These laws must have been set by someone."*

Space exploration is governed by Laws of the Universe which work in such precise harmony that we can totally rely on them. We could not make the correct calculations for space travel and be able to land on the moon if the solar system was not in timely accord.

Both creationist and evolutionary scientists are in agreement that the universe had a beginning, in line with the natural laws of physics. Consequently, if something had a beginning then it must have had a first cause – *cause and effect* being a basic scientific principle. As the cause is always greater and superior to the effect, the first cause of creation must have dominion over the effect of the universe.

Because the origin of the universe is governed by scientific law with planetary arrangements highly systematic and the laws of nature well organised, then the initiation of that first cause must be comprised of hyper-extraordinary capability. As intelligence is manifest in creation, that first cause must be comprised of Supernatural Intelligence, hence a Universal Creator. As love and emotion is present in creation, then God is also characteristic of those attributes, hence the God of the Bible. Evil exists in the world, but as the biblical God is one of justice and love, this abomination must come from another source, hence Satan the perpetrator of Evil. Atheists accept, as they must, the principle of cause and effect relating to all aspects of science, except for the origin of the universe, thus ignoring scientific law.

The endurance of intricate life systems is confirmation of the reality of a precursor to those life systems. The unification of nature displays and validates the presence of Divine Genius and the magnitude of our universe secures the belief in a higher quintessence than man. Ungodly minds cast a blur on this observation, but a willingness to attempt some degree of understanding may lift this veil from the mind's eye, opening up a vision of reality and belief previously closed to one's perception. A closer look will reveal the truth of God as manifest in all aspects of nature and the universe.

Though it may be difficult to prove with 100 percent certainty that God exists, the logic we draw from the vast amounts of quantitative evidence for creation, gives us the confidence and assurance to firmly believe in Him. The evidence recognised through nature and our universal environment illustrates why Christian faith is not blind, unlike the followers of evolution who are forced, by lack of corroboration, to adopt a totally blind faith. God's jewel in space exhibits His handiwork with awesome fascination and impels the spiritually liberated mind to be enthralled and engulfed by it. The finger of God is seen in every leaf and every flower. You can perceive it in every pair of eyes. You can feel it in every heartbeat and every breath of air. It is observed in every creature on earth and in every form of life. The awesome wonder of a Master Creator is evident in each handful of soil and in every drop of garden water (a living world of microscopy in itself). The presence of God is manifest in each sunrise and every sunset. Why are they so magnificently beautiful if not for the joy of man?

Intelligent design can be the only explanation for the structure, complexity and function of the brain, heart, eye and the molecular cell. It is rational to conclude that properties in the life-blood running through our veins could only have been formulated by Divine thought. Is it coincidence that the elements in our bodies are the same as elements in the soil of the earth? This is no chance occurrence from a biblical viewpoint: *"And the Lord God formed man of the dust of the ground, and breathed into his nostrils the breath of life; and man became a living soul"* (Genesis 2:7).

The manifestation of God's creation is experienced in every birth and renewal, in the depths of our emotions and in all corners of the natural world. Those who fail to recognise and appreciate the signs of their Creator are poor in spirit: *"For the invisible things of him from the creation of the world are clearly seen, being understood by the things that are made, even his eternal power and Godhead, so that they are without excuse"* (Romans 1:20). God's trademark is stamped in every niche of His invention. Biblical directive warns us against the peril of denying the existence of God: *"The fool hath said in his heart, there is no God"* (Psalm 14:1).

Noah's Footprints

Just as the Garden of Eden is wrongly viewed by many as a fairy tale, so too is the account of a worldwide flood. Christian geologists have no difficulty explaining a catastrophic worldwide deluge, and linking the aftermath to the composition and structure of the earth's surface. The geological features of mountain, hill, canyon and valley are easily defined and clarified within the time frame of a few thousand years and not the millions of years claimed by the evolutionists. The fossil record is the result of what you would expect to find, centuries after a global watery catastrophe. Sea shells and fossilised sea creatures are routinely found on mountain summits including Mount Everest, the highest mountain on earth, and there are lines of Noadic induced water marks all over the earth as seen in canyons, ravines and cliffs.

Back to Two

Reversal assessments of the world's population going back to zero, has been conducted with remarkable results. The present global population count of six billion in reverse, taking into account wars and famines etc, has been estimated to reach zero between four and five thousand years ago. This is in line with Noah's flood around 4,300 years ago, when the only survivors on the ark were Noah and his wife, their three sons and three wives.

The world population by Roman census at the time of Christ was approximately 250 million. The reducing trend from the numbers of people in the pre-flood period (1,700 years) would inevitably arrive at one male and one female, in line with the biblical book of Genesis. This practical analysis validates the account of Adam and Eve, coherent with the existence of an initial Creator. In summation, the history of global population development is coefficient with the statistical laws of demography. If man had finalised a supposed evolving process a million years ago, he would have been intelligent enough and had ample time to record his presence in some kind of calligraphic composition. The assumed million years of human evolutionary history is a blank, as it would be, granting it never happened.

If we are to believe the evolutionary claim that man reached his present form one million years ago, then the population of the world would have reached saturation point many thousands of years ago. It has been calculated that if man had begun to reproduce a mere 50 thousand years ago, the present population of the world would be so great that human beings would have all been standing shoulder to shoulder, occupying every square foot of land on earth, several millennia ago. Biblical chronology tells us that God created the world around 6,000 years ago. Taking into consideration all assessments of global population growth, the present population of six billion inhabitants fits absolutely with this evaluation.

In the first two chapters of this book, I have provided a moderate but adequate amount of information to meet the requirements of discerning readers looking for truth. Ultimately, we have the free will to make judgements, but the choice is not difficult. The bottom line in our search for confirmation of our origins rests with two alternatives. We can choose to believe that in the beginning nothing exploded or that God invented everything.

In man's relentless search for the meaning of life, there is no better explication available to him than the foundational book of Genesis in conjunction with the sacrifice at Calvary and the resurrection of Christ. A deep perception of this threefold union of doctrine reveals a scope of understanding which no other agency can provide. Genesis explains our beginnings and fall from God's grace. The cross reveals our reinstatement into God's favour, and the resurrection establishes the promise of eternal life. If earthly death is the end, there is no meaning to anything.

The differentiation between creation and evolution enfolds with the following resolution:

- We cannot, in the ultimate degree, prove the existence of God neither can we disprove His existence.

- We cannot prove the theory of evolution but we can disprove it.
- Therefore, alternatively and indirectly, we can be secure in our belief of the existence of God.

That God exists is a decisive systematic calculation. Those who find themselves in conflict with spiritual matters are evading self-belief by their own disposition. God will not allow us an understanding of His revelation, unless we exercise our free will in the direction and practise of humility. Pride is the antithesis of humility and therefore pride is the barrier to enlightenment.

The crucial decision facing each individual is whether to live one's life under the banner of evolutionary faith, which offers nothing, or the covenants of God which offer so much:

- If we believe in God and we are wrong, we will never know.
- If we believe in evolution and we are right, we will never know.
- If we believe in evolution and we are wrong, we are in grave trouble.
- If we believe in God and we are right, we will have eternal life.

Ponder for a moment the suppositions, A and B:

(A) If we had a 3,000 year old history book explaining in detail and step by step, how the evolutionary process worked with good evidence for support, then we would be happy to accept it without question.

As it happens, the opposite is the case:

(B) We are fortunate to have a 3,000 year old history book that informs us implicitly how the earth, universe and all life came into being, naming Adam and Eve as the first created inhabitants.

If the unbelievers of this world would have no problem accepting (A), why do they have so much difficulty in accepting (B)?

SUMMARY

Ten Golden Truths

1. Frauds and Hoaxes by Evolutionists: Over the past 100 years they have been numerous. These perpetrations are testimony to the absence of proof or worthwhile evidence on behalf of the Theory of Evolution.

2. Converts from Evolution to Creation: Many evolutionary scientists have converted to Creationism. They would not do so unless the evidence for creation greatly outweighed their previous beliefs.

3. The Big Bang Theory: Scientifically false. An explosion cannot produce order and precision, as demonstrated by the solar system.

4. Transitional Fossil Chains: None found out of the 100 million fossils unearthed. This nullifies Darwinian criteria.

5. World Population Growth Reversal: Assessment counts of today's six billion inhabitants reverting back to two originally created people 6,000 years ago, taking into account wars, famines, natural disasters and Noah's flood, are compatible with the book of Genesis.

6. *Human Genetics:* The cell, eye, heart and brain are too complex to have happened out of nothing.

7. *Man's supposed evolutionary history of one million years:* Totally blank trace.

8. *Alleged Evolutionary Line:* From nothing to particles to > atoms > molecules > fish > reptiles > birds > mammals > apes > humans. This process contravenes the law of biogenesis, has never been observed and is based on fabricated assumption.

9. *DNA and Mutations:* Modern scientific analysis proves the impossibility of any evolutionary correlation.

10. *The Solar System and Universe:* A finely tuned clockwork mechanism of infinite proportions and synchronisation demands the input of Infinite Intelligence.

Power to Choose

Having scrutinised the evidence on behalf of Creation and Evolution in order to determine the way of truth, each individual must rest on their acquired acumen. Where does the balance of quantifiable information take you? How does your intuition advise you? No philosophy or religion has all the answers, but we can evaluate the preponderance of facts to discern truth and meaning. We have found that design and purpose is inherent in our sun, moon and earth, and we know that complexity of design demands the input of a master designer. Christ has revealed to humanity that He is the designer builder of all creation and man can safely place his trust in the God of the Bible as Saviour of mankind.

Where does this leave the fish to ape to human philosophy? With the numerous advances in science demonstrating the function of the DNA molecule and the negative performance of mutational activity, I am confident that Charles Darwin would be happy to admit that his theory is dead. Science has returned the monkey to its rightful place. As captain of our own ship, it remains for us to steer in a safe and trusted direction. Free will is a powerful gift which directs the course of our earthly life. We can choose to follow an evolutionary dead end. We can ignore biblical guidance and hide under the cloak of agnosticism, or we can follow in the footsteps of Jesus Christ. No one is forcing us, but the choice we make will determine our eternal status.

CHAPTER THREE

Our Troubled Earth

The world today is steeped in perplexities which have never been known before. Despite the advancement of man throughout the past century, with huge improvements in technology and living standards, unrest abounds worldwide. There are more wars than ever before, as nation rises against nation, natural disasters occurring with escalating frequency, and governments that are impotent in their attempts to solve the problems of social conflict, poverty and famine. Family breakdown is commonplace, neighbours are at war with each other, the divorce and abortion statistics are frighteningly high and the global-wide drug problem is unsolvable. Crime and immorality are rampant, prisons are bulging at the seams, unruly children are on the increase and not least of all we have the problem of terrorism. How significant are these trends? Do we accept them as a natural progression or should we seek a broader explanation?

In western society, people prefer to ignore world crises. We assume the freedom and benefits of an affluent lifestyle and conduct our lives with the expectation of an unchanging continuum. Through the media we observe incessant mayhem in the surrounding world, never to imagine how we could become seriously involved.

Through religious television media channels, we frequently hear discussions on the subject of the end-times or last days as they are often called. Christian leaders and biblical scholars seemingly agree that we are now living in those end-times as prophesied in the Bible. Some biblical prophetic indicators are mentioned above and there are many more, pointing to impending world strife for the inhabitants of our earth.

Do you ever ask yourself why the world is the way it is? Have you ever asked yourself why, from the moment of birth, you begin the process of ageing and decline, and why, during the ageing process you are continually prone to all types of illness and disease, eventually having to succumb to infirmness and death in a mere 70 or 80 years, and in many cases earlier. Are you curious to know why we are forced to suffer the forces of nature and foul weather? Why must we tolerate the effects of natural disasters such as hurricanes, tornadoes, earthquakes, volcanic eruptions and tsunamis? Why are we subject to all manner of accidents? Are you bemused at the conflict amongst nations and why civilized human beings are so hostile to each other?

If you believe in a caring and loving God as the Divine Creator, you will wonder why He should have made His creation this way, affording the sceptics amongst us every opportunity to blame Him for the sufferings of the world. The Bible informs us that God loves His creation and every human being He ordained to be born. It does not make sense that He should have made a defective and troublesome world when He could have made it quite perfect.

You are quite justified in thinking: If God did make the world this way, then He cannot be much of a God. There must be an explanation. If you were able to question Him about this, what do you suppose His answer would be? I think it could be something to this effect: "Dear child, have you not read my Bible? I have told you clearly, that I made the world very good." *"And God saw everything that he had made, and, behold, it was very good"* (Genesis 1:31). The words "very good" clearly eliminate all the unpleasantness and suffering in the world today. They discount wars, human discord, natural disasters, illness and disease, worry and strife, and more significantly they rule out death, our biggest enemy.

The Perfect Earth

If we are to accept God's word as written, it follows that in the beginning the world must have been perfect, as stated in the Bible. If we disagree then we stand accused of denying the word of God. Many people conceive the Garden of Eden to be a fairy tale, though it makes sense that God would have made His creation an ideal place to live for the people He loves.

Adam and Eve, being genetically perfect in God's initial creation, were the most unblemished human specimens ever to exist. There is no reason why their Maker would have fashioned them any other way. Their environment was equally untarnished. The air they breathed was pollution free and their food and water was essentially pure. Adam and Eve were destined to live forever, as were all their descendents, to dwell in an environment of perfection, to live in complete harmony and never to die. It makes sense that an all powerful, loving God would have planned and constructed such a faultless creation in the beginning.

Biblical chronology informs us that Adam lived until he was 930 years old and consequently his many children, possibly hundreds, must have lived to an equally long age. If you find this difficult to accept, maybe you could ponder the fact that since the fall of man, after Adam sinned, the whole of humanity has been born genetically imperfect, which is why we are prone to illness, ageing and eventually death. We are defective from our mother's womb and this precipitates our short lifespan.

If we were born like Adam, genetically perfect, and like Adam we could constantly dwell in a perfect environment, there is no reason why we would not live in a prime state of health for many hundreds of years or maybe forever, if God so desired. Before the fall, there was no such thing as death. But thereafter, God cast Adam and Eve out of the garden and from that moment, humanity was thrust into decline, proceeding to physically die.

For 6,000 years, while man has progressed in numerous technical spheres, genetically and biologically he has fallen into continual descent. The life span of mankind has run concurrently with this decline, as specified in biblical chronology. Adam's life of 930 years and Noah's life span of 950 years were not to be repeated. After the flood we see a sharp dip in the time of Abraham and Isaac who lived to be 175 and 180 years old respectively, succeeded by Moses and Jacob who managed to endure for a mere 120 and 147 years.

Records now show that in the 21st century, one in three of the world's citizens do not live past the age of 60 years of age and very few reach the century mark. The fall and decline of mankind is not only physical but also apparent throughout the natural and cosmologic world. Compared to the time of Adam, our food and water is putrid, our weather conditions are disastrous, and our immune systems woefully weak. The earth's magnetic field, which protects our bodies, is becoming progressively ineffective, inflicting on the earth's biological systems an ever decreasing life term, as man is forced into a permanent struggle against degeneration and early death.

What went wrong?

You may be eager to ask why the perfect creation had to go wrong. That is a very poignant question but the Bible can explain. God did in fact create a perfect world with a perfect environment, for highly refined people to live in harmony forever, as of course He would. Evangelists have been telling us for a long time that something did go wrong with the wondrous creation of God. This is when Evil entered our world in the name of Satan. Contrary to what some people think, Satan is not some mythical demon but a real spiritual being that dwells amongst us causing untold havoc, pain and suffering. From the moment that Satan tempted Adam and Eve into sin, thus breaking the law of their Creator, the world has been pitched into battle against Evil and we are all part of the struggle of Good, against the terrors of Evil.

In the aftermath of the fall of man, we are now compelled to forage our way through a disturbed existence, the price we must pay for our sinful ways, and imperfection is now inherent in our entire way of life. Satan takes full advantage of our frailties, but knowing that his time is limited and in order to gratify an insatiable revenge, his mission is to drag as many souls as possible away from God, eventually to be destroyed along with himself and his followers. This is the entity of Evil which is manifest in our world. The powers of darkness will rampage amongst us if we allow them a foot in the door. The present earth is a battle ground in the fight for the souls of men.

But God is not happy with the state of His creation and is

about to restore it to its former glory. Mankind must be patient a little longer, as we do not know exactly when Christ will return to complete His mission of defeating Satan and restoring an earthly and everlasting peace.

If a master builder were to erect a palatial mansion, his pride and joy, and vandals were to wreck it, the builder would desperately want to restore it to its former pristine condition. This is the situation that God holds in restraint at the present time. The earth, His creation, His pride and joy has been wrecked and He patiently anticipates the moment when He must step in and reinstate it to its former glory.

I can hear you ask, if God is all powerful, why did He allow this devil to cause so much trouble? Why did He not destroy him? Why wait 6,000 years or more to put matters right? These are searching questions which are bewildering to sceptics and Christians alike, but we must remember that God is good and perfect. He cannot permit Himself to act in any kind of devious way. His ways may be strange and inscrutable to His people on earth but they are always fair and righteous. God could destroy Satan any time he desired, but the God of justice and truth must give Satan a fair trial. Democracies around the world are known to give criminals an unbiased hearing even though they are often certain of their guilt. God has imparted His ways of justice onto us and will certainly abide by them Himself. Satan has been convicted, but his sentence is pending and only the Father knows when the time is right for the devil's internment.

The Bible tells us that with God, a day is but a thousand years and a thousand years is but a day. God is outside of time, in fact He created time. We may have difficulty understanding it, but the 6,000 years of man's earthly occupation is nothing to our Maker and we must have faith in His preferred time-scale.

Satan the Deceiver

As for Satan, we must remember that he betrayed God's trust. Satan, once Lucifer, was a beautiful angel gifted with free will, but he chose to misuse it against God. He was endowed with great power and beauty, but his power was to be misdirected for Evil rather than Good. Lucifer became jealous of God's impending creation of mankind and thinking be was better than God, he plotted to take over God's throne. When you hold the highest position, there is often someone who wants to replace you. Just as some unscrupulous Vice-President may have the ambition to be President and would contrive any devious measure to achieve his goal, Lucifer conspired to dethrone his God.

When the wicked plan failed, Lucifer was banished to earth in the form of a serpent. To further his punishment, God removed the devil's legs, forcing him to slither on his belly, and henceforth, snakes were to be the most abhorrent creatures known to man.

The Bible informs us that the vengeful Satan lured Eve into tempting Adam to eat of the forbidden fruit, so perpetrating the first sin of mankind (original sin). Since this period, known as the fall, our ideal world has been reduced to imperfection, hence our troubled earth, and because the whole of humanity has inherited Adam's sinful nature, suffering and death has been inherent in all people on earth. Romans (5:12) explains: *"Wherefore, as by one man sin entered the world and death by sin; and so death passed upon all men, for that all have sinned."*

Having assumed Adam's sinful nature, degenerate man has been forced to struggle and endure the anguish of 6,000 years, accumulating in the stress, turmoil and suffering forever threatening our everyday lives. Collectively, all the sins of humanity are responsible for the chaos, suffering and strife of the living world.

There has never been an innocent man born, but for Jesus Christ, so we cannot solely blame Adam for the genetic decline and regression of subsequent generations. We are all guilty of various sins and must endure the penalty which God has inflicted upon us. The burden of transgression is on our shoulders and on every single person who ever lived. Those who blame God for the sufferings of humanity should perhaps look to themselves for the part they have played, no matter how small they perceive it to be. God loves the sinner but hates the sin, just as we love our children but hate their devilish behaviour. Why should we expect our lives to function in harmony, if we are constantly entrenched in the habit of breaking God's laws, or ignoring Him altogether? From God's perspective, He is looking down on degenerate and ungrateful inhabitants of His creation who reject His covenants and the promise of eternal life.

No Innocents

There are no sinless people on earth. Even blameless children will eventually grow up to become sinful adults. One sin is abhorrent to God and we have all sinned: "*As it is written, there are none righteous, no not one*" (Romans 3:10). The world is tainted with our iniquities and this is why we deserve to be dammed forever. That is the bad news. The good news is that God loves us and has sent His son Jesus Christ on a rescue mission for all humanity.

So the battle rages as it has done for 6,000 years. God verses

Satan, Good against Evil. Every human being is a part of this battle and we are being tested daily, minute by minute. Are we on the side of Satan or do we walk with God? There is no middle ground, as the Bible once more directs us: *"So then because thou art lukewarm, and neither hot nor cold, I will spew thee out of my mouth"* (Revelation 3:16). What a frightening thought for those who prefer to sit on the fence and ignore spiritual beliefs and Godly ways.

The devil is continually casting explosives into the workings of our lives. He is the master destroyer, the master deceiver, the master liar. He knows our weaknesses and knows exactly how to manipulate us. Living a Godly life does not make us immune to his influence, and we must always be on our guard, but it does give us armour and strength as a measure of protection. Our struggle for honour is a tug of war between God's grace and Satan's deadly poison, and sadly, too many of the unwary amongst us are playing straight into his wicked hands. Evil men of war, dictators, terrorists and many wicked people are under his influence, casting their nets of human devastation, causing untold suffering in the most abhorrent manner. Satan thrives on conflict, hate, violence and murder, engulfing the perpetrators in acts of frenzy. It is not unusual for murderers, having emerged from their spell of Evil, to be utterly bemused at their sinful deeds. They often do not know where their Evil came from, only that they were possessed by some unknown force. Being blessed with the grace of God would have immunised both themselves and their victims from such a path of destruction. Our world is influenced by strong spiritual forces with the power to infiltrate our lives, but not always for the good. We are tempted into wicked ways by Satan, not by God: *"Let no man say when is tempted, I am tempted of God; for God cannot be tempted with evil,* neither he tempteth any man" (James 1:13). The weakness of man under satanic inducement is responsible for the many afflictions that plague humanity. We live in a fallen world tainted by our infractions and the resulting chaos continues to affect the natural creation as well as our personal lives.

Prayer is man's great weapon against demonic ways. Prayer calls on God for protection, and though prayer is not always answered in the way we hope, God will deliver in the way he knows best: *"The Lord is far from the wicked, but he heareth the prayer of the righteous"* (Proverbs 15:29).

The book of Job tells us how Satan challenged God. Job tells us that Satan, so to speak, threw down the gauntlet in front of God, telling Him that mankind would follow satanic ways rather than a Godly path, and that man would become wicked rather than righteous. When we observe the troublesome state of the world around us and contemplate on the foolishness of human endeavour, it is not difficult to understand why Satan was so confident.

Satanism is Escalating

By the state of worldly upheaval, it would appear that Satan is winning and well he may be. If you are aware that Satan is in fact the present ruler of earth as the Bible states, then maybe you could harbour a better understanding of the tribulation that man is forced to encounter: *"And the great dragon was cast out, that old serpent called the devil, and Satan, which deceiveth the whole world; he was cast out into the earth, and his angels were cast out with him"* (Revelation 12:9). Satan is constantly pitting the rancorous nature of people against one another, and this is exactly what we observe in all spheres of life. God gifted His human creation with loving sex, but Satan has stained it with lust – one of the six deadly sins, often leading to jealousy, violence and murder.

21st century man is not embracing his Creator as he should. Humanism in a secular framework is rampant and God is being rejected with distain in the world of anything goes. Increasingly, man wants to make his own rules and forage his own path, but this is precisely the mistake that Adam made in the Garden of Eden, with monumental consequences spanning 6,000 years. Recent generations have run out of control and one gets the feeling that we are about to encounter a backlash under the most horrifying circumstances.

Increasing pressure is being placed on governments to relax the laws on abortion, drug taking, homosexuality, euthanasia and a host of moral issues which contravene the laws of God. Ungodly people, often in high places, are incessantly pushing the envelope, gnawing away at Christian standards. The values that bond society are forever being questioned, with the sanctity of marriage being invariably under attack. Biblical guidelines are being ignored, consequently society is suffering and Satan is rubbing his hands at the turmoil he is able to generate. The mayhem continues today and into tomorrow and man cannot bring peace on earth while Satan is around. Governments and world powers have failed and will continue to fail in their attempts to bring stability to our planet. Little do they realise that the real enemy, who thwarts every attempt at world peace, is not defiant man, but man under satanic domination.

Satan rules by an unseen stealth aimed at the unwary who may be oblivious to his presence.

This troubled world is destined to continue until Christ comes again to obliterate Satan out of existence. Christ came the first time to redeem the soul of mankind. His second coming will be to defeat Satan and rule over a new creation. For 6,000 years, history has shown that man is not capable of ruling himself and he must rely, once again, on Christ to come to his rescue.

Have you ever asked yourself why people are compelled to work for a living? The structure of daily exchange demands that most of us are forced into work which is tedious and often soul destroying: *"Thou shalt earn thy bread by the sweat of thy brow,"* said the Lord, but this was not the situation in the original world that God created. In the Garden of Eden, the work that God assigned to Adam was healthy, enjoyable and rewarding and that state would have continued but for his dishonourable fall from grace. The Bible tells us: *"And the Lord God took the man and put him into the Garden of Eden, to dress it and to keep it"* (Genesis 2:15). It was God's desire for Adam and Eve and their descendents to cultivate and enhance His new creation, so that subsequent generations and eventually the entire world could continue to revel in an earthly paradise. But for Adam's disobedience, the work of mankind would have been a pleasure instead of a task. In the original and perfect world which our loving God created, that makes perfect sense, and so the drudgery of work since that time is part penalty for the sins of mankind.

After the curse, God told Adam unreservedly: *"Because thou has hearkened unto the voice of thy wife and hast eaten of the tree of which I commanded thee, saying, Thou shalt not eat of it, cursed is the ground for thy sake, in sorrow shalt thou eat of it all the days of thy life; thorns also and thistles shall it bring forth to thee, and thou shalt eat the herb of the field; in the sweat of thy face shalt thou eat bread, till thou return unto the ground"* (Genesis 3:17-19).

The repercussions of sinful generations have been manifest

in the pathetic state of our troubled earth. We are entombed in an earthly prison where riots, wars, chaos and unrest have become an integral part of world culture. We are compelled to shoulder the collective blame for our iniquities and must continue to endure until Christ calls a halt. Our fractured world is a far cry from the original work of our Creator.

The air that we breathe is polluted and our food and water contain toxins. Because of sin, we have to cope with thorns, weeds and pests among the beauty of our gardens and we are compelled to toil and sweat for a living. Instead of embracing our fellow associates, we needlessly declare war on each other, as the minds of the ungodly become stained with envy, greed, hatred and revenge. Mother Nature is becoming increasingly hostile and children are rebelling as never before. We have to face illness, disease and pain from every source and stress is so prevalent in our everyday lives that psychosomatic illnesses are escalating to frightening levels. 6,000 years after his genesis and despite his rise in opulence, man is in a permanent state of civil and social unrest. If we are fortunate to extend our lives to three score years and ten, we must eventually surrender to an inevitable death, our most fearful enemy. Is this the world that a loving and caring God created? The Bible says no.

Why are world governments failing to deliver permanent global stability? Countless peace treaties have been signed during the last 100 years but all to no avail. It should not be surprising that we are unable to live in a peaceful world, when mankind is separated from God through sin.

After the First World War, the League of Nations was set up to ensure no more global conflict, but in a very short time the world was embroiled in yet another worse catastrophe. After the disaster of World War Two, when 55 million people lost their lives, the United Nations came together in a union that was intended to finally bring about world harmony. Over half a century later, we are still struggling to live in peace. While there has not been a Third World War yet, there have been many smaller but exceedingly bloody wars around the globe, collectively resulting in a bigger loss of life than the two global conflicts combined.

World leaders cannot prevent wars because of the dark powers which grip all nations. Quite often it takes little to instigate hostilities. Why is this, when man prefers peace? During the last century, over 200 million people have been killed in armed conflicts. These are great victories for Satan, but though he has won many battles he will not win the ultimate and decisive war.

If national governments could listen to the message of the Bible, they would be better informed of the obstacles which hinder the means of achieving world peace: *"The way of peace they know not, and there is no judgement in their goings; they have made them crooked paths; whosoever goeth therein shall not know peace"* (Isaiah 59:8).

While man is helpless in achieving a semblance of global coordination, biblical prophecy informs us exactly how peace will eventually arrive on earth, but that is for another chapter. The great danger, which nations face today is not politically motivated, nor is it about land, sovereignty or ethnic differences. The global battle we face is religiously based and it is out in the open for all to witness. The monster on our doorstep is encapsulated in the East verses West agenda, in Extreme Islam verses Christianity, in terrorism backed by some Arab nations against Europe and America.

This battle has been raging for centuries and is gaining momentum. We cannot defeat terrorism, only Christ can accomplish such a feat. The controversy ravaging our planet is of a spiritual nature and is about "Which God is the real God?" The impending conflict of extreme Islam verses Christianity will converge, in the not too distant future, into one almighty clash, with a Third World War being the assured outcome. Two thousand years after Christ, the world is sitting on a time bomb. Satan has his tail up and is ready for action, but happily for mankind this demon and his followers will be fighting a losing battle. After the next and ultimate worldwide combat, they are doomed to oblivion.

Taking a glance at global events, we can clearly see a world crisis brewing, with the roots of this conflict firmly embedded in the Middle East. This region is and has been embroiled in localised warfare for a long time while western society looks on. Why are world leaders so concerned about this volatile region and why are they trying so desperately to bring about stability? They know that within the unstable Middle East there lies the trigger to a third world conflagration, in the centre of which lies the tiny country of the democracy of Israel.

If you doubt that satanic influence is the root cause of world strife, avail yourself of the history of the Jewish nation. Why has anti-Semitism prevailed for so long? Why have the Arab countries surrounding Israel commanded such hatred of the Jews? In Psalms 83:4 of the Old Testament, we are told of present day dissention concerning God's chosen people: *"They have said, Come, and let us cut them off from being a nation; that the name of Israel may be no more in remembrance."* In line with biblical premonition, Arab leaders have openly voiced their satanically driven desire for God's people to be hurled into the sea and wiped off the face of the earth. Advocates of world peace could not hear a more disconcerting statement.

After suffering the atrocities of the Holocaust, losing six million of its citizens, Israel was given sovereignty by the

United Nations Assembly on 14th May 1948. The very next day they were attacked by Egypt, Jordan, Syria and Lebanon. What is the reason for such animosity and why have Israel and the Palestinian people been in conflict for the past 60 years? The roots of these troubles linger over the long standing dispute concerning the rightful ownership of the land of Israel. Palestinian rights go back many centuries, but the right of Israel to proclaim sovereignty goes back 4,000 years to the time of Abraham: *"In the same day the Lord made a covenant with Abram, saying, Unto thy seed have I given this land, from the river of Egypt unto the great river, the river Euphrates"* (Genesis 17:8). (Genesis 15:18) also claims: *"And I will give unto thee, and to thy seed after thee, the land wherein thou art a stranger, and all the land of Canaan* (now Israel), *for an everlasting possession; and I will be their God."* Do the adversaries of the Jewish nation really want to challenge the decisions of God?

The Israelites, in the aftermath of the Exodus, settled in the land known as Canaan about 3,500 years ago, long before a Palestinian presence. The controversy hovering over this disputed land can never be solved by politics or diplomacy, and because the issue is central to the avoidance of world upheaval and destruction, all nations remain suspended on the brink of Armageddon, ad infinitum.

If ever anyone was involved with Godly blessings on one hand and satanically induced brutality on the other, it was the Jewish race. Having survived and prospered, surely of Divine assistance, they are constantly at the centre of world attention, their survival and democracy being pivotal to world unity.

At the time of writing, Israel is once again embroiled in conflict, but this time within her own country. Having relinquished territory to the Palestinian people for the purpose of peace, in retaliation she finds herself attacking that same territory in order to stave off terrorism. But the propaganda war is more damaging to Israel than any armed conflict. The primary aim of her terrorist enemies is a relentless campaign to deliberately incite other nations against Zionism. This is the ugly face of anti-Semitic hostility which is rocking the boat of world stability, causing nations to turn against this beleaguered country. Informed Christians believe that they are witnessing the initial signs of biblical end-time prophecy as it emerges before their eyes.

I must stress that all Arabic people do not hate the Jews. Over one million Palestinians have lived side by side and in harmony with the Jewish fraternity for a long time. They are an integral part of the democracy of Israel. But those who attempt to abuse the Jews are inviting the wrath of the Almighty, as God's covenant promise to His chosen people still holds fast today: *"And I will bless them that bless thee, and curse him that curseth thee"*(Genesis 12:3).

The Arab/Israeli discord could be settled at a stroke, if anti-Semitic resentment was quelled. Arab nations have an abundance of land to offer their Palestinian counterparts, allowing both the Israelis and Palestinians to live in permanent peace. Could it be that, instead of helping to rehabilitate their Arab cousins, governments from the surrounding states of Israel wish the Palestinian people to be a thorn in the side of Israel? If this is true the objective is working. It is apparent to biblical scholars that wicked forces are seeking to cause mayhem throughout Israel, the heart of God's earth.

History is littered with regimes that have harmed the Jewish race and paid the penalty. The Assyrians, Babylonians, Persians, Romans, Ottomans and the Nazi Party have all disintegrated after years of persecuting these tormented people. Not least of all, the proud and valiant British Empire, once guilty of its own Jewish persecution, is now but a shadow of its former self. No democratic power can ignore this small piece of real estate. The land of Israel is at the nerve centre of our troubled earth.

Love your Neighbour

We are commanded by God to love our neighbour for a very good reason, but this does not merely refer to the person living in the adjacent house. Our neighbour can be anyone with whom we come into contact and especially those in trouble who we are able to help. Perpetrating lies about one another is so commonplace in our disgruntled world, that many consider it to be noble rather than sinful. God's word tells us: *"Wherefore putting away lying, speak every man truth with his neighbour, for we are members of one another"* (Ephesians 4:25).

Why is this commandment of God so important? After our devotion to God, He has named it as the second most important: *"Thou shalt love the Lord thy God with all thy soul, and with all thy mind; This is the first and great commandment, and the second is like unto it; Thou shalt love thy neighbour as thyself; On these two commandments hang all the law and the prophets"* (Matthew 22:37-40).

If human kind could collectively make an attempt to obey such an important law of God, the affect on our habitat would delight our Creator to such an extent that maybe the problems facing humanity would somewhat abate. Satanism feeds on man's animosity towards his fellow associates, and the Wicked One knows precisely how to provoke our negative emotions, such as envy and jealousy, into conflict with our colleagues.

Friendly neighbours are a priceless commodity as it allows, on our door step at least, a continuing harmonious and Godly existence. If neighbouring countries made a similar effort to be more amicable to each other, our world would not be so troublesome.

This planetary domain is steeped in error and we no sooner solve one problem when another takes over. Whether we are a politician or a plumber, a large part of our day is utilised in thinking about or working on our problems. This was not the case in the original creation. With the devil's wicked power and ascendency waiting to perpetrate every corner of our lives, problems are a constant irritation. We wonder why life lets us down and why we are subject to so much stress. We vainly try to build a Utopian existence in a protected environment, but life's imperfections and failures constantly thwart our endeavours.

As we probe for solutions to our stricken planet, we see conflict and pain in every quarter. There is no doubt that strange forces are at work, infiltrating our lives in ways that we do not understand. The biblical account of a once ideal creation, with sorrow and death thrust upon us because of the disobedience of man, is a fitting explanation of the circumstances which we see afflicting our daily lives. The sensible answer is to turn to the God who created us, but too often the evolutionary bogey is used as an excuse to not believe in Him.

Can we see a miraculous formula which gets rid of the pain while retaining the pleasures of living? The gospels (meaning good news) say yes, but we need to practise the virtue of patience. God's Bible informs us and world events indicate that the ultimate and idyllic scenario, preceded by a period of distress as in the end-times, may not be far away.

CHAPTER FOUR

The Bible has Answers

What does the Bible have to say about the contentious issues of the previous chapters? Those who are familiar with Christian theology and biblical doctrine know that the book of Genesis not only refutes the concept of evolution, but demonstrates exactly how God constructed our planet. No scientific method can determine the origin of the earth or mankind, but we do possess the greatest history book ever written which relays to us in detail how life and the universe originally emerged. The earthly home of mankind is not some out-of-shape object floating aimlessly through space. Our planet avidly displays a marvel of design and engineering, a formation of immense constitution and organisation, strategically placed in the cosmos for a purpose. Believers embrace the biblical logic which demonstrates an earthly purpose for the will and pleasure of the Creator. The magnificent and diverse nature of living things bear witness to the presence of a perpetrator, not only of those living things, but also the subsidiaries. The book of Genesis gives a clear explication of the essence of living organisms.

Why does the earth hold such oceanic quantities of water? Life needs water. Why is there warmth? Life needs warmth. Why do we breathe air? Life needs air. Why does the earth supply natural food? Life needs food. I could go on. The Bible explains our origin, our presence and our destiny. God's book reveals the scientific principles which allow life to function and why man has the promise of eternal continuation. No other religious book conveys such a detailed clarification of the object and meaning of the birth to death cycle on Planet Earth.

God not only created the universe, He presented us with a manual in order to understand why. I have found that many good people who seek knowledge of the existence of God have never taken the opportunity to understand His guide book, or alternatively, listen to those who are expert in the Christian teachings of biblical direction. Just as a car manual provides the owner with a comprehensive explanation of how to operate it, the Bible is a reference book of information from God in how to conduct our lives.

Some people view the Bible as a boring old book compiled by frail old men with white beards, but they are widely mistaken. Moses for example, editor of the book of Genesis, was highly educated and a great leader, commanding a place as one of the great historical figures. Luke is hailed by many as one of the great historians of all time. Other biblical writers range from judges to kings, all hand picked by God to pontificate His words to mankind. Many authors of the Bible were prominent men of their day, who wrote with authority and conviction, and their writings were only accepted after great scrutiny, as being divinely inspired.

Since the Bible was finalised almost 2,000 years ago, it has become established as the greatest and most successful book of all time, and one has to be either naive or ungodly to dismiss it as just an old book. The Bible is prospering today more than at any other time in history having been translated into more than 1,000 languages, and the sales of this dynamic book top the million mark each year. Countless numbers of people the world over have placed their faith in the written word of God and reaped great reward. The Bible demands such unique and unequalled authority that courts of law have no hesitation in using it to trust the conscience of its witnesses in solemnly swearing to truth. No book by man could command such a high status of importance and supremacy.

The Bible Speaks

The Bible is a series of books. First of all, it is a Holy Book accepted by two billion Christians (one third of the world's population) as the inspired word of God. It is also a history book, the most significant history book ever written. The Old Testament communicates a clear, step by step account of our origins and a chronology of events leading up to the time of Christ. The New Testament tells us about Christ's ministry on earth and informs mankind of what we can expect concerning our eternal fate. The Bible is a guide book, directing us how we are expected to live our lives and also a reference book to remind us of God's teachings. It is exclusively the best advice book ever written with counsel and instruction touching every area of our lives.

Divinely Inspired

Most importantly, the Bible demonstrates a wealth of evidence that no one else but God Himself could have authorised it. Yes, it was physically written by man, but many historians and biblical scholars are adamant that man alone could not possibly have composed the Bible from his own knowledge. They are convinced that the Bible, having been coordinated in such a cohesive, balanced and informative way, must surely have been inspired by God, as every one of the writers professed.

Many authors of the Bible, having later reread what they had written, were amazed at the words in front of them, nor did they have any conception that their writings would eventually be incorporated into the famous book which the world holds in such reverence. Assembled by some 40 authors over a period of around 1,600 years, the 66 books of the Bible blend together so perfectly, that it is accepted as the greatest literary work of all time, incidentally an easy accomplishment for God.

Writers of the Old Testament frequently mentioned their awareness of the inspiration of God in their lives. Some of the New Testament authors were not accomplished writers and were quite worried when Christ instructed them to go forth and devise the Scriptures. The fact that they did complete the scripts is confirmation of Divine inspiration, as they were not capable of writing without expert assistance. Christ assured His disciples that there was no need to worry, as they would receive Divine guidance to write the words of God: *"The holy spirit will put words in your heart."*

In the Epistle of Paul to the Galatians (1: 11 and 12), he writes: *"But I certify you brethren, that the gospel which was preached of me is not after man; for I neither received it of man neither was I taught it, but by the revelation of Jesus Christ."*

The Holy Bible is the most powerful, distinguished and successful book of all time. Other written works pail into mediocrity in comparison to the Bible and even the best of books fall short in status and popularity. Written works come and go but the Bible continues to endure. This great book commands a pinnacle of its own in the literary world and its influence on mankind far surpasses any other work conceived by man. The Bible is the rock on which God's words are engraved and they cannot become extinct. Neither God nor man will allow its doctrine to wane.

The Bible speaks

How do we know that the Bible is true? We know because (unlike other religious books) the Bible has proven to be astonishingly accurate in science, archaeology, geology, cosmology and biblical prophecy, having stood firm against immense critique over the centuries. One quarter of this amazing book is composed of biblical prophecies laid down some hundreds of years before the events, and up to this present time almost 80 percent (over 1,400) have come true exactly as foretold.

These vital facts are ignored and unpublicised by atheists, evolutionists and the secular media of today:

- Hundreds of years before the event, the book of Micah (5:2) predicted that the promised Jewish messiah would come and be born in Bethlehem.
- The book of Isaiah (7: 14) predicted the virgin birth.
- A vivid account of the crucifixion of Christ was foretold in Isaiah (53) and (Psalms 22).
- Psalms (22:16) tells of the piercing of the hands and feet of Jesus.
- Psalms (22:18) relates how the soldiers gambled for the garments of Jesus after the crucifixion.
- Psalms (34:20) explains why the soldiers decided not to break the bones of Christ (a common practice after crucifixions).

We know from written history that every one of these prophetic events took place with amazing accuracy and there are many more prophecies concerning the life and death of Christ, which also occurred precisely as stated in the Bible.

The most poignant biblical prophecy concerning the Jewish people has been fulfilled in my lifetime. In the Old Testament, the verse of Nehemiah (1:8) relays the word of God directly to the Jewish race: *"If ye transgress, I will scatter you abroad among the nations,"* and centuries later, He did exactly that, using the dominance of the Roman Empire. We know that the Jewish race was dispersed by the Romans and scattered throughout the world two thousand years ago. On 14th May 1948 against impossible odds, many claim that a God-ordained miracle took place. The United Nations passed a resolution to hand Israel back to the Jewish people. This event can truly be described as miraculous and is in line with the prophecy of Isaiah (66:7-8), that Israel would be reborn in a single day.

Prior to 1948, the very thought of the Jews ever possessing a land of their own was an impossible dream. The thought of Russia voting in favour of the Jews living in their own country was unthinkable, yet at the United Nations assembly the Russian vote was crucial. They shook the world by consenting to the re-establishment of the state of Israel after a 2,000 year exile, thus fulfilling biblical prophecy in this present age: *"I will gather you from the nations, and assemble you out of the countries where you have been scattered, and I will give you the land of Israel."* (Ezekiel 11:17). What the world deemed impossible for two thousand years was now a reality, but the Bible knew it was destined all along.

During the exile, other nations of the world had become extinct, but not the Jews. Being forced to live apart, far and wide for two millennia, they retained their identity, their language and their culture (a miracle in itself) and now they had taken possession of their sovereignty. In a very short time, they established themselves as if they had never been away. Who can deny that Divine providence was playing a part?

In the early part of the 20th century, Israel was a virtual wilderness with scant pockets of population. At this present time, 60 years after the Jewish re-occupation and despite repeated conflict with neighbouring Arab states, Israel is rich in agriculture and exports the finest produce to the far corners of the world. Tel Aviv, its capital, has developed into a vibrant and modern city. The progress of the Jewish people in such a short period of time has been greatly admired by other nations, but was foreordained in Amos (9:14): *"And I will bring again the captivity of my people of Israel, and they shall build the waste cities, and inhabit them, and they shall plant vineyards, and drink the wine thereof; and they shall also make gardens, and eat the fruit of them."*

Among her many achievements, Israel has developed her own nuclear capability (justified as a deterrent for her protection), and has assembled one of the most efficient defence forces in the world. On the map, Israel is but a slither of land bordered by several Arab countries and the new owners knew that strong defence was necessary for her survival, in order to suppress the anti-Semitic hostilities of the surrounding states.

Many people firmly believe that the Jewish nation could only have survived by Divine assistance as prophesised. God's chosen people of the Bible will not and cannot be vanquished, being a vital part of God's earthly plan, soon to be accomplished, as you will read later.

Science and the Bible

The scientific accuracy of the Bible cannot be denied. Scientists once believed that the earth was flat, while the Bible was telling them that it was a sphere: *"It is he who sitteth upon the circle of the earth..."* (Isaiah 40: 22).

The Bible was explaining gravity when gravity was undefined: *"He stretcheth out the north over the empty place, and hangeth the earth upon nothing"* (Job 26:7).

Our earth's hydrological cycle was declared long before man was sure of its rotation: *"All the rivers run into the sea, yet the sea is not full; unto the place from whence the rivers come, thither they return again"* (Ecclesiastes 1:7).

The book of Genesis informed us that the universe had a beginning well over a thousand years before the scientists had worked it out. The sequence of God's creation in seven days as stated in Genesis, is in direct line with scientific conclusions of the modern era. The beginning, with an earth in darkness, followed by light and atmosphere, then sun, moon, stars, land and vegetation, after which came sea creatures, birds, animals and finally man, is universally accepted by science in the exact order stated in the Bible. Scientists could have saved themselves much work and deliberation and arrived at these conclusions decades in advance, if they had initially sought information from The Book.

Many examples show that the Bible and science go hand in hand. As God invented the laws of science, this should not be surprising. The great scientist, Isaac Newton once stated: *"No sciences are better attested than the religion of the Bible."*

Archaeological finds have confirmed biblical theology and a great deal of biblical theology has instigated archaeological finds. Archaeology, geology, cosmology, and other areas of science are in complete accord with biblical creed. In contrast, not one law of science is compatible with evolutionary projection.

Though Bible prediction has proven itself to be true over and over again, there are still those who seek to deny its authenticity. Jesus himself stated: *"If I have told you earthly things, and ye believe not, how shall ye believe, if I tell you of Heavenly things."* He was explaining that if we are reluctant to believe what is staring us in the face (the physical facts of creation), we are granting ourselves little chance of believing in spiritual matters.

The Bible Endures

Why has the Bible survived, triumphant and successful for two thousand years? Over the centuries, generations of kings, emperors and the ungodly have tried to wipe all traces of the Bible from existence. All attempts have failed, despite threats to many people being commanded under penalty of death not to own one. In past centuries, it was not uncommon for Bibles to be piled up and burned in their thousands, but all to no avail.

This great book is a thorn in the side of many godless people, who find it disconcerting in their attempts to cope with its doctrine and durability. Instead of embracing it, they vainly try to ban it from society, and to this present day, one is prevented from taking a Bible into certain countries.

The Bible has faced so much opposition since its completion, there is a strong belief that it could only have survived centuries of time by Divine assistance. God will not allow His words and teachings to be destroyed.

The Guide to Living

Our democratic laws and social values are governed by this informative book and civilisation is guided by it. Our seven day week was founded on biblical example and we know from trial and error that man performs most efficiently by working for six days and resting on the seventh. Any alternative working time scale has proven to be unproductive. If we work for five days or less then we lose capacity. If we work for seven days or more without respite, we become overtired and less efficient.

Exodus (23:12) reaffirms the book of Genesis, that man and working animals should adhere to the seven day system of living: *"Six days thou shalt do thy work, and on the seventh day thou shalt rest; that thine ox and thine ass may rest, and the son of thy handmaid, and the stranger, may be refreshed."* God could have created the world in any time schedule that He wished, but He chose the seven day week as an example for man to emulate. Man has followed this path, which has worked with great efficiency. God, who created us, knows what is best for us.

Where did our laws originate? – The Bible. Where were our moral standards conceived? – The Bible. Where did our social values come from? – The Bible. The arrangement for living was laid down by God's word for the proficiency of mankind, which has proven to be necessary for man to live in peace and harmony with his fellow associates. God defined these laws for a purpose and man has wisely adopted them, but frequently has been unsuccessful in keeping them. When we flout the statutes of God we can expect strife and discord. When we attune to them we reap the benefits.

Wars are caused by man breaking the rules of the Bible. Man commits crime by disregarding the commandments. Family breakdown and social conflict are caused by ignoring biblical guidelines, while arrogant and unruly youths play havoc with society in ignorance of the Holy Book. Having no Godly course to follow, they run amok with their own lowly standards, devoid of respect and dignity.

Abortion, drug addiction, homosexuality, alcohol abuse and crime are all contrary to the laws of God as declared in the Bible. These laws were given for the betterment of mankind and it is easy to observe the adverse affects on society when they are so flagrantly contravened.

Sin and Suffer

If the whole of humanity could somehow attune themselves to God's wishes, maybe the entire world would unfold in a haven of serenity. Contrary to what some people choose to believe, God is not responsible for the troubles of this world – sinful man under satanic influence is the culprit. God is tearfully taking vengeance on the earth for man rejecting Him and deciding to follow his own path.

When children incessantly ignore their parents and do as they please, the result is trouble and conflict in the family home. Conversely, if they habitually obey their parents, the family will live in peace and harmony. The same principle applies to God and His earthly people. God is our Father, we are His family and we are paying the price of disobedience to His standards. The stress of living is collectively man made and we are little different from an unruly family. God has the authority to tell us how to live in the world that He created for us. His instructions for living are clearly defined in the Holy manual and we ignore them to our detriment.

Because of The Fall, our entire world has laboured under God's curse: *"For we know that the whole creation groaneth and travaileth in pain together until now"* (Romans 8: 22). The restlessness of the human spirit is an affliction we must endure: *"And not only they, but ourselves also, which have the first fruits of the Spirit, even we groan within ourselves, waiting for the adoption, to wit, the redemption of our body"* (Romans 8:23).

In order to understand the Bible, it is necessary to be of willing heart and mind: *"The natural man receiveth not the things of the Spirit of God, for they are foolishness to him, neither can he know them, because they are spiritually discerned"*

(1 Corinthians 2:14).

No matter how intelligent we are, the knowledge of God will evade us, unless we humble ourselves and willingly move towards Him: *"Draw nigh to God, and he will draw nigh to you."* (James 4:8). Those of us who are unable to seek or enter into the truth of God may forever dwell in ignorance of Him. God has made Himself known through His book, and it remains for each individual to make use of the gift of free will bestowed upon us, in order to seek and understand what He wants from us.

The Bible holds a wealth of answers to our doubts and queries. We may not fully understand everything, but that is no reason to doubt our faith, in fact, it should be complementary to our faith. Compared to the string of certainties concerning a Godly faith, we carry only a handful of doubts. I believe that God denies us a little knowledge in order to test our faith. Christians can be confident in their values, while harbouring a certain amount of mystification. An unshakeable faithfulness to biblical truth will overcome any ambiguity which we may occasionally encounter.

God has placed His book in every corner of our habitat. The Bible is made known to all mankind and it will be difficult for anyone to harbour the excuse that they could not acquire knowledge of His decrees for living.

If the Bible writers were not genuine then we have no veritable way of approaching life and our purpose becomes meaningless. It would mean that mankind has no relevance. Human insight tells us that there must be a reason for the existence of life and I have heard many non-religious people agree with this appraisal.

Ignorance of God and His Bible can plunge the human soul into deep depression, while enlightenment of a Godly presence can fill one with hope and exhilaration. We are not staid, unemotional creatures, but spiritual in nature, as well as physical and our varied emotions would not be possible without a Divinity to place them within us.

The Biblical Flood

Evolutionists try to portray the worldwide flood of Noah as a fairytale, though Genesis (7) devotes no less than 24 verses to give us an account of its feasibility. The Ark that Noah and his family built was over one length and a half the size of a soccer field with three decks suitable for accommodation. There was ample room for fifteen thousand animals or more. It is estimated that the huge floating hotel for livestock would have taken Noah and his family at least 50 years to build. The epic voyage becomes more practicable if you consider that Noah would have taken only small and healthy young animals on board.

Earth's geology is strictly compatible with a worldwide catastrophic deluge having taken place no more than a few thousand years ago, as the Bible states. Fossil discoveries carry a direct linkage towards the aftermath of the flood of Noah and reflect what one would expect to unearth as a result of such a cataclysmic watery event 4,300 years ago. Scientists recognise that few fossils are being formed in present times, re-enforcing this view.

Love Each Other

The most earthly piece of advice that can be found in the Bible is to love your fellow humans and to this extent God has placed it as the greatest of His commandments. Why is this? Consider the repercussions of ignoring this advice and observe the resulting chaos reflected in the state of our communities. Neighbourhoods in today's society are rife with conflict and the knock-on effect abounds far and wide. For no good reason, neighbours declare war on each other, with some feuds lasting for decades. Very often the initial spark is trivial, while the trail of human grief proliferates. A friendly neighbour is a Godly commodity while we live side by side on this earth, and God will reward such people when they meet up with Him.

The Bible tells us that strife and conflict are detrimental to one's health and bad for the heart: *"A calm heart is the life of the flesh, but envy the rottenness of the bones"* (Proverbs 14:30). *"A merry heart doeth good like medicine; but a broken spirit drieth the bones"* (Proverbs 17:22). Modern-day physicians are now confirming what the Bible has been saying for 2,000 years.

From the Sermon on the Mount, Jesus commanded: "Love your enemies." This philosophy is inconceivable in our time and we wonder why there is so much discord in the world. How ignorant we are of some basic humanitarian laws. Like attracts like and hate attracts hate. If you scowl at someone they will most certainly scowl back, but if you smile at someone they will surely smile back. Smiling is contagious and if we could make more use of it with our associates, the world would be a happier place. The more we have ignored biblical guidance, the worse our world has become. Biblical words are God's instructions.

In our prayers we should always consider the plight of the Jewish people and their quest for peace in the Holy City, in fact we are requested by the Bible to do so, under the promise of God's blessing: *"Pray for the peace of Jerusalem; they shall prosper that love thee."* (Psalm 122:6).

The Bible is universally accepted as the greatest book of all time and the integrity of its authors is sacrosanct. Fulfilled biblical prophecies emphatically confirm its truths, and since its completion 2,000 years ago, no person or regime has successfully discredited the wisdom within its pages. God's biblical narrative has been scrutinised and misinterpreted many times, but the basic message of our origin, man's fall from grace and his salvation through Christ remains steadfast. Jesus preached that we must not argue over words. What we believe in our hearts will determine our final judgement.

Written by the infallible word of God, through the hand of man, the Holy Bible commands authority in every province of our lives.

CHAPTER FIVE

Jesus is the Way

The most significant period in the history of mankind spanned the years in the life of Jesus Christ, and no other human being has left such a profound and lasting influence on the nations of this earth. Just as the sequential events of history confirm the bygone reality of great figures, Jesus Christ established Himself as the most renowned figure of all time.

Who was this famous man? Most importantly, He professed to be God. That assertion must have been an astonishing revelation to the people who knew Him and to others who heard of Him. At this present time, two thousand years later, over two billion people (one third of the human race) and billions prior to this period, firmly believe that He was telling the truth. Why are they so sure? Why has their faith endured for so long?

It is difficult to perceive how two billion people and the billions before them could be deceived into thinking that Jesus Christ was God, if He was merely man. During the last two millennia, since Christ's reign on earth, many millions have suffered persecution and were prepared to sacrifice their lives in honour of this man named Jesus.

Most Christians, of course, are born into the faith and you might say that they worship Christ as a matter of routine. That is true as children, but children become adults with an independent free will and are able to formulate their own judgements. They are able to decide for themselves from historical evidence and the world around them, what in their opinion is truth.

The two billion Christian believers in Jesus Christ, alive today, cover a very broad range of intellects. Among them are many millions of high intellectuals, including scientists in every field, also professors, authors, the clergy and numerous others with Ph.D. qualifications. Can they all be wrong? The French philosopher Jean Louis Pascal stated: *"There lies a God shaped vacuum in the heart of every person, which only Jesus Christ can fill."*

We cannot discuss the life of Christ without further biblical scrutiny, so initially we need to know what the Old Testament, written long before His time, has to say about His mission.

Prophecies Fulfilled

The Old Testament contains over 100 prophecies foretelling the coming of the Messiah, together with His ministry, crucifixion and resurrection, which were all fulfilled to the letter. These prophecies were predicted hundreds of years before Christ's reign on earth and could not have been manufactured. Christian leaders, biblical scholars and many historians are in agreement that biblical prophecy has proven itself to be genuine.

Micah (5:12) predicted that a Jewish messiah would come and be born in Bethlehem: *"But thou Bethlehem, though thou be little among the thousands of Judah, yet out of thee shall he come forth unto me that is to be ruler in Israel; whose goings forth have been from of old, from everlasting."*

Isaiah (7:14) told that this messiah would be of virgin birth: *"Therefore the Lord himself shall give you a sign; Behold, a virgin shall conceive, and bear a son, and shall call his name Emmanuel."* Such a prediction must have been fiercely ridiculed up to the time that it actually happened.

Psalm (41:9) and Zechariah (11:12) speak of the betrayal of Christ by a friend for money, no doubt referring to the apostle Judas: *"Yea, mine own familiar friend, in whom I trusted, which did eat of my bread, hath lifted up his heel against me - And I said unto them, If ye think good, give me my price; and if not, forbear. So they weighed for my price thirty pieces of silver."*

Psalm (22:16) foretold of the piercing of Christ's body: *"For dogs have compassed me; the assembly of the wicked have enclosed me, they pierced my hands and my feet."* This prediction is quite startling, as the piercing of criminals was not used until centuries after the time of writing.

Psalm (22:18) describes how the soldiers would gamble for Christ's clothing after the crucifixion: *"They part my garments among them, and cast lots upon my vesture."*

Psalm (16:10) clearly refers to the resurrection of the dead Christ: *"For thou wilt not leave my soul in hell; neither wilt thou suffer thine Holy One to see corruption."*

Psalm (68:18) explains the ascension into heaven, the last act of Christ, having completed His task of redemption for mankind: *"Thou hast ascended on high, thou hast led captivity captive; thou hast received gifts for men; yea, for the rebellious also, that the Lord God might dwell among them."*

These prophecies are but a few of the many, concerning the life of Jesus during His earthly mission and give credence to the biblical authority of the Passion. The pre-eminence of the Jewish Messiah has now survived with dignity for two thousand years. Past centuries are littered with Christian persecution, which continue to this day. Martyred in the name of their Lord, men and women, particularly in the first century, were willingly tortured and butchered to death rather than renounce their faith in this Holy Man. The only conclusion one can draw from their courage is that they firmly believed in their God incarnate, and they must have had very legitimate reasons to lay down their lives for their convictions. Many early Christians had first hand knowledge of the miracles and resurrection of Jesus Christ.

Jesus must have been God or He was the biggest fraudster the world has ever known. Is it possible to fool all the people who knew Christ, into believing He was God, if He was not? I do not think so, as it is difficult to see how that could be accomplished. Biblical scholars would undoubtedly deem the feat to be impossible. The words of Christ, as He was hanging in agony from the cross and about to die, are not the words of a fraudster: *"Father forgive them, for they know not what they do."*

Genuine Miracles

Christ convinced people that He was truly God, in the only way possible – by working miracles. If He had not performed miracles, no one would have believed that He was God. But many people did believe that He was God, so He must have delivered the miracles as written in the scriptures. Having affected the miracles of which we are familiar, He must have been God. Here we have a circle of confirmation, backed by the written word of history, from people who were present at the time, that Jesus was the Son of God. Atheism is eager to remind us that miracles are against the laws of nature. But they overlook the fact that our Creator invented the laws of nature and consequently He can operate outside those laws. Miracles only exist as earthly phenomena. In Christ's arena they are not miracles but the norm.

Every day during the catholic mass, a miracle of transubstantiation takes place, where the host and wine is transformed into the body and blood of Christ: *"Verily, verily I say unto you, except ye eat the flesh of the Son of man, and drink his blood, ye have no life in you. Whosoever eateth my flesh, and drinketh my blood, hath eternal life; and I will raise him up at the last day"* (John 6:53,54). This mystery of faith, inaugurated at the last supper, is scoffed by many, and though Jesus Christ ascended from earth two millennia ago, those who wish to receive Him, like the apostles, are blessed with His presence at the Eucharist.

The Holy Trinity, often used as ungodly ammunition by atheists, is another mystery of faith. Though the Bible does not mention the word trinity, the Father, the Son and the Holy Spirit were all preached by Christ as one God. Though it may be a mystery to our finite minds, Christians are happy to embrace the teachings of Christ. God does not lie.

The supernatural accomplishments of Jesus were so convincing that the authorities at the time became fearful of His popularity. The growing adoration of Christ was undermining the status of the Roman hierarchy and it was this conflict which steered the way to the crucifixion. Performing miracles gave Jesus great power and the only way the authorities could eradicate that power was to get rid of Him.

Jesus Christ is the most glorious, distinguished and exalted figure of all time and no one else throughout history has been elevated to the rank of Christ the King. So why did Jesus have to die on the cross? The simple answer is – To save each and every one of us from damnation. And why are we all damned? We are damned because we are sinners: *"For all have sinned and fall short of the glory of God"* (Romans 3:23). The whole of mankind has inherited the sin of Adam, and through our sinful natures, we are condemned to an earthly and everlasting death: *"Wherefore, as by one man, sin entered the world, and death by sin; and so death passed upon all men, for that all have sinned"* (Romans 5:12).

God did not want His unrighteous creation to perish, and in order to save them He was compelled to make a sacrifice. The Bible tells us that without the shedding of blood there is no remission of sin, and because an animal was inadequate to compensate for the enormity of man's transgressions, the sacrifice demanded a perfect human offering. As Christ was sinless, He became the perfect sacrificial lamb.

Our Redeemer had the power to descend from the cross any time He wished, but His Father had sent Him on a mission and the purpose had to be ignominiously fulfilled. No matter how sanctimonious a life you may think you have lived, you could not have been saved except for the blood of Christ. Why do you think that Christians hail Him as Our Lord and Saviour. The person who truly recognises the sanctity of the Cross is truly saved, and provided we repent of our sins from the heart and hand them over to God, He will gracefully forgive us. The price for our iniquities has been paid in full, to those who accept it: *"God so loved the world that he gave his only begotten Son, that whoever believes in him shall not perish, but have eternal life"* (John 3: 16).

Man is gifted with ethereal intuition and there is no excuse for lack of Godly awareness. Truth is written in the Holy book and we insult God by evading it. Ignorance of our earthly law is no defence in court, neither can spiritual darkness be used in abdication of our knowledge of Jesus Christ.

How often have we heard someone ask: "If God exists, why

does He not let us know?" We come to know God through His Bible. This great book is God speaking to us and continually beckoning us to follow Him: *"I am the way, the truth and the life; No one comes to the Father, but through me"* (John 14: 6).

What a wonderful God our Creator is. He created us, He loves us, He shed his blood to save us from the fires of hell, and all He asks in return is for us to believe in Him. If we continually shun His counsel, then we cannot say that we deserve His Kingdom.

The Risen Christ

Jesus not only suffered and died on the cross for the sins of humanity, He also rose from the dead, the final proof that He really was God. Can we be sure about this? Yes, we can. If Christ had not risen from the dead then Christianity could not and would not have been born. The resurrection is the very foundation of Christian Faith. Romans (1:4) confirms: *"And declared to be the son of God with power, according to the spirit of holiness, by the resurrection from the dead."*

The dead body of Christ was never found, having been sealed in a tomb and guarded by roman soldiers, who were instructed to do so under penalty of death. The resurrection, the most consequential event in the history of the world had just taken place and people at the time were aware of it. They knew that the future would be changed forever. After Jesus had died on the cross, His disciples were very disillusioned. The man they believed to be God had just passed away before their eyes.

They went back to their boats to become fishermen once again, as there was nothing else they could do. Without the resurrection, all of the people who believed in Jesus would have simply forgotten about Him or labelled Him a fraud, and His life would have disappeared into the ashes of time. The resurrection, the most powerful event in antiquity, is now the most established fact of history.

Can you imagine what the disciples experienced when they first saw the risen Christ? Here He was standing before them alive and well, the holes in His hands and feet clearly visible. Even the doubting Thomas was eventually convinced. Their Lord had defeated death, and by defeating death He was demonstrating to the whole human race that those who believe in Him will also defeat death and rise again to dwell for evermore in His Heavenly Kingdom.

It is not difficult to realise how the disciples were inspired and motivated into leaving their fishing nets once again, and to go forth preaching the word of their Lord and everything He had taught them. They knew with certainty that He was God, which bestowed on them the incentive and desire to drive forward and preach to the known world. Christianity was born.

The disciples were not the only people who witnessed the presence of the risen Christ. In the few weeks after the resurrection, while He remained on earth, Jesus made himself known to around 500 people. They were also pioneers in spreading their first-hand experience of the risen Messiah. Christianity and the message of our salvation were made known to every generation thereafter.

Who killed Jesus?

Who is responsible for the death of Christ? This question has been a bone of contention for centuries. Some people blame the

Romans who performed the execution. Others say it was the Jews who gave their consent. The truth is that the whole of mankind shares the guilt. Every human soul who has sinned is responsible and that encompasses each one of us. Because of our personal disobedience to God's laws, we have all placed Christ on the cross. Jesus opened the door to salvation, but before we are privileged to walk through that door we are compelled, for a time, to accept and suffer an imperfect and troubled existence.

Why has the legacy of the ministry of Christ endured for 2,000 years? Why has it not drowned in the depths of time? The truth of Jesus Christ is with us because the Holy Spirit dwells amongst us and permeates our lives. If it were otherwise we would be like animals, but man has a soul and spirit that elevates him to a higher rank than other creatures on earth.

The Bible teaches that we cannot possibly be saved by our own good works: *"Not by works of righteousness which we have done, but according to His mercy He saved us, by the washing of regeneration, and renewing of the Holy Ghost"* (Titus 3:5).

The only way we could have earned salvation by our own actions is to have lived a perfect life, but man has found that to be impossible, as no one has been able to adhere to the commandments adequately. God laid down His rules for living to expose our failings, so that when we fall short of His perfection we are obliged, for our own good, to concede to His mercy.

If man was capable of an absolute righteous lifestyle, there would have been no need for Christ to have rescued us. His final words, "It is finished" exemplify the task that the Father had bestowed on Him. Satan was vanquished and the door was ajar for man to repent of his sins and place his faith in the sacrifice of Calvary. By shedding His blood, Christ opened the door to man's redemption and those who wish to follow Him have to willingly walk through that door: *"And almost all things are by the law purged with blood; and without shedding of blood is no remission"* (Hebrews 10:22). The first Adam brought sin and stain to the soul of man, but the last Adam (Jesus Christ) cleansed it on man's behalf.

To be saved, we must personally humble ourselves with the act of repentance and believe from the heart that Christ shed His blood in atonement. Those who believe they can merit eternal life by their own works and deeds are elevating themselves beyond their station: *"But we are all as an unclean thing, and all our righteousness is of filthy rags, and we all do fade as a leaf, and our iniquities, like the wind, have taken us away"* (Isaiah 64:6).

Our moral failures are compatible with the Bible in showing us how inadequate we are in keeping the commandments of God, and it is understandable that if we are to attain the ultimate prize of eternal life, we must rely on a sympathetic God to help us achieve what He has prepared for us.

No Other Way

There is no other pathway to salvation except through surrender to the blood of Jesus Christ: *"For God so loved the world that he gave his only begotten Son, that whosoever believeth in him shall not perish, but have everlasting life"* (John 3:16). *"Believe on the Lord Jesus Christ, and thou shalt be saved, and thy house"* (Acts 16:31). This suggests that not only believers are saved but also their family.

The Romans devised the act of crucifixion to ensure a maximum amount of pain for the longest duration without killing the victim prematurely. Christ paid the ultimate sacrifice for us, but being God, His divine powers kept Him alive until all blood was drained from His body. When the soldier pierced His side, the last drop of blood was followed by water. This alone proved that Jesus was indeed God as no man could have retained consciousness and endured pain to such an extent, as he would have lost consciousness long before such endurance. Maybe it was this perception that prompted one of the soldiers who had assisted in the crucifixion, to fall on his knees and cry out that they had surely crucified the true God.

Now, the way was open for the redemption of God's fallen people. Christ had foiled Satan from the Cross and it was up to man to recognise the fact. Prior to the crucifixion, sinful man had forged a huge separation between God and himself, but God in His love and mercy and by making the ultimate sacrifice had taken a huge step towards us, in order to narrow the gulf. Man was now able to reunite with Christ in order to replenish the union that originally existed between The Creator and His Created. The whole of mankind was now obligated to walk through the gate of salvation and take the vital step closer to God.

Man is being challenged to bury his pride and not throw the sacrifice which Jesus endured, back in His face. Those who deny Christ are antichrist in nature and place themselves in danger of damnation. They expose themselves to the clutches of satanic inducement and are open to temptations which are manifest in daily situations. In retaliation, we do possess armoury to stave off satanic power. Two things which Satan hates and which weakens his approach are the Sign of the Cross and the name Jesus. These two forces are the invincible enemy of Satan and he becomes powerless against them.

Like Satan, man in general is a proud creature. The devil's

sin of pride was responsible for his downfall and the pride of mankind is the predominant stumbling block in his need for the acceptance of Jesus Christ as his Redeemer. Pride forms a barrier to spiritual understanding in the mind of man. Humility opens the door to enlightenment and spiritual truth, but sadly, the virtue of humility is a rare commodity in our emancipated world.

Being merely religious does not guarantee salvation, as no one is capable of keeping the commandments faultlessly: *"There is none righteous, no not one"* (Romans 3:10). Being saved by allegiance to the Cross does not mean that we are free to indulge a loosened lifestyle. We must strive to keep the commandments even though we are destined to fall short of perfection.

"God loves a trier" is true to the Bible and though we may continue to stumble, it is an ungodly act to give up.

"The Christian message is for those who have done their best and failed." *Anon.*

By placing our banner on the Christian mast, stained by the blood of Christ, we acknowledge the ultimate sacrifice which Christ suffered on our behalf. The blood of Jesus has wiped our slate clean: *"Though your sins be scarlet, they shall be white as snow"* (Isaiah 1:18). What a wonderful promise by our God of the Bible, and all He asks in return is our confidence in Him. The greatest man that ever lived suffered and died for the love of mankind, including those who have ignored and rejected Him.

Why do non-believers, sceptics and also some Christians fail to understand that despite our multitude of transgressions, the price for all the sins of humanity has been paid in full? How many people attempt to lead sanctimonious lives under the impression that their good deeds will see them through?

It is folly to amble through life under a self-appointed halo: *"For by grace are ye saved through faith; that not of yourselves; it is the gift of God; not of works, lest any man should boast"* (Ephesians 2:8 and 9).

Those who reject Christ as their Saviour must ultimately pay their own price. You can hand your sins over to God who has mercifully redeemed you or you can elect to bear the burden yourself. We are gifted with a free will to make choices and there is no middle ground: *"He that is not with me is against me; and he that gathereth not with me scattereth abroad"* (Matthew 12:30). Having been saved by the shedding of blood, our place in God's eternal home is determined by our efforts to obey His commandments. I feel that many people are under the illusion that if they become devout, their quality of life will diminish. While following a Godly path may be a little restrictive, the benefits of love, hope and peace of mind will far outweigh any constraints on life.

Among the many Gods that man has decided to follow, none other than Christ has been willing to rid him of his iniquities. The Bible tells us that we cannot put our trust in any other God: *"Neither is there salvation in any other, for there is none other name under Heaven given among men, whereby we must be saved"* (Acts 4:12).

Unlike animals, man, on a higher level, has been gifted with the endowment of free will. He is gifted with the intelligence to use his free will, and he is blessed with the free will to use his intelligence for good or ill. This confirms an unbridgeable chasm between creature and man which cannot be explained by any evolutionary concept. The gap is too large.

How often do we stop to consider that the greatest of our earthly achievements is miniscule compared to the goal of eternal life? No prize on earth can compare. Earthly pleasures and accomplishments wither and fade, but the Kingdom of God will never fade. If we are able to invoke the motivation to achieve our worldly ambitions, surely we can drive ourselves to acquire a permanent Utopian existence and fulfil God's purpose for us. Christ emphasised the ephemeral state of worldly preoccupations and obsessions while advocating the permanence of Heavenly joy.

We are a unique human creation placed on earth for a purpose and God knew every one of us long before we were born: *"But the very hairs of your head are all numbered"* (Matthew 10:30). Mankind is part of the creation that was wrecked but will soon be restored. To be part of that restoration, we are asked to take the hand of Jesus Christ and never let go. Satan is forever in waiting, ready to divert us from a Godly path, the moment we let our guard down. Our directions for the journey to God's house are signposted in the Holy Book. Jesus Christ is the way, the one and only way.

There is nothing wrong with earthly accomplishments. They are admirable. But they should not take prominence over our Heavenly goal. We can live agreeable and fulfilling lives through work and play without ignoring the rightful path. Earthly aspirations may be pursued with guile but what is the value if not with God: *"What does it profit a man, if he were to gain the whole world and suffer the loss of his own soul."* (Mark 8:36).

No matter what our station in life may encompass, the Heavenly honour is open to all, and the least of God's people are equipped to challenge for a place in His Kingdom. Wealth and fame, so elevated on this earthly stage, can forge a huge stumbling block in achieving eternal life: *"But many that are first shall be last; and the last first."* (Mark 10:31). In the eyes of God, meekness and humility are more worthy attributes than earthly riches.

A quiet assurance and persistence in a Godly direction will consummate the once broken relationship with Our Redeemer and win for us the Heavenly Crown. Human inadequacies do not hinder us from achieving our heavenly goals while meekness in our failures may well be our strength:

There is no prize on this earth, no trophy, no medal that can remotely equal the prize of eternal life. Victories in this world of whatever worth are temporary. The eternal victory is permanent and everlasting. We do not have to acquire fame or wealth. The plain and simple ordinary you competes daily for the greatest prize of all. Take comfort in yourself, that in your humility and in your niche as a modest human being, you do possess the criteria to compete and win with glory, the ultimate victory. (George Di Palma.)

Earthly death is not the end of our existence but the interim. Just as leaving school is not the termination of our lives but the end of an apprenticeship and the beginning of a future lifespan. Physical death is merely the culmination of an earthly probation period, allowing us to move on and take our place in the Kingdom of our Creator. As children's education usually determines their station in adult life, the manner in which we conduct our lives will have a bearing on our place in the house of God.

Death is but a pause in the early time of eternity and we must enter the interval with unyielding faith. Though we learn many truths through the Bible and the life of Jesus Christ, God does not tell us everything. This is why faith is paramount to our salvation. What we lack in known facts, we must replace with loyalty of faith: *"For by grace are ye saved through faith; and that not of yourselves; it is the gift of God"* (Ephesians 2:8). Endurable faith is part of the great test.

Jesus said to His apostles: *"Blessed are those who have seen and believe, but more blessed are those who have not seen and believe,"*

(John 20:29). Even though we were not present to witness the miracles of Jesus for ourselves, if we trust in His word, our faith in Him will be rewarded in ways that we are unable to contemplate.

Revelation (3:20-21) announces this message from the heavens: *"Behold, I stand at the door and knock; if any man hear my voice, and open the door, I will come in to him, and will sup with him, and he with me. To him that overcometh will I grant to sit with me in my throne, even as I also overcame, and am sat down with my Father in his throne."* God has promised His faithful people great things if they walk the true path and persevere till the end. From God's perspective, the important thing in life is not what we achieve but what we overcome.

Devout people do not attend church because they are perfect, they worship so that they may become perfect even though they will never achieve it. Striving for piety in the face of an earthly struggle with secularism is devout in nature, but persistence is the key to success. We must fight the good fight and keep the faith. Perseverance wins the Crown.

Through our trials and tribulations, Jesus is always at our side. Most Christians are familiar with the footsteps poem that touches at the very heart of our relationship with Christ. The last verse is sufficient to kindle the spirit: *"The years when you have seen only one set of footprints, my child, is when I carried you."* This divinely inspired verse vividly expresses that we are not alone in our earthly journey. Unfortunately, there are those who wish to ignore the Holy presence and prefer to tread their own path, but sadly, the more you choose to move away from God the further he will depart from you. The essential message of salvation is to be born again. This means ridding ourselves of the inhuman attributes incorporated in our negative emotions such as hate, envy and revenge. (Matthew 5:44) tells us: *"Love your enemies, bless them that curse you, do good to them that hate you, and pray for them which despitefully use you, and persecute you."* This is what Christ asks of us.

Place yourself in the position of a criminal who is facing a life sentence. Out of the blue, a man comes forward who is prepared to serve the complete term of incarceration on your behalf. Later, he humbly asks that you appreciate his offer and wants you to visit him once every week for an hour. Wouldn't you be eternally grateful and only too pleased to conform to his request? Jesus Christ intervened to save every human soul from an eternal life sentence of damnation, and all He asks in return is for us to believe in Him and visit Him in worship for one hour in each week. Isn't this a small gesture in reciprocation of the enormous sacrificial deed of Calvary?

Ticket to Eternity

Can you imagine placing all of your past, present and future sins in one box, together with a letter of repentance. Can you imagine taking that box to the personal secretary of Jesus Christ? Can you visualise receiving an acknowledgement and receipt for those sins? Well, that receipt is what you will need to enter Paradise. When you stand at the entrance to the gates of Heaven, an angel will ask you for a receipt for your sins, stamped and sealed with the blood of Christ. On that receipt must be the signature of your Saviour, signed: "Your sins paid in full, Jesus of Nazareth." Only then will you be permitted to enter the Kingdom of God.

CHAPTER SIX

The Return of Our King

Christian leaders are unanimous in their teachings that this present age is the time of the end or last days according to biblical doctrine. What makes them so sure? To find the answer we need to go back 2,000 years and listen to the words of Jesus Christ the One who knows. Prior to His ascension into Heaven from the Mount of Olives, Christ revealed some very significant future events to his apostles. As He was God He was qualified to do so. He promised that He would return to earth a second time at some undisclosed date, but He informed them that the world would experience definite signs when His second coming was imminent.

Until the 20th century those signs were dormant, but in recent decades there appears to be some evidence that what the world is now witnessing seems to coincide with the prophecies of which Jesus Christ spoke, before His departure from earth two millennia ago.

Jesus spoke of wars, famine, earthquakes, world unrest, an increase in crime, family breakdown, the spread of immorality and much more. Jesus said that when all these occurrences begin to escalate, His return would be near. He told His disciples that these events would begin as birth pangs, signifying that they would gradually increase and become more severe with the advancing years.

Let us examine a few of these signs and prophecies. Prior to World War One, there was relative peace and stability throughout the world compared with present day conflicts. The Second World War quickly followed and since then the unfolding mayhem does seem to assimilate the end-times pattern to which Christ was referring.

The most significant prophetic event to have taken place in the last century is the return of the Jews to their homeland Israel in 1948. Ezekiel (37:21) foretold of this almost miraculous development: *"Thus saith the Lord; Behold I will take the children of Israel from among the heathen, whither they be gone, and will gather them on every side, and bring them into their own land."* The Bible emphasises that this one prophetic episode would initiate the end-time events and that does appear to be the case. Isaiah (66:8) reiterates how Israel would be reborn in a day, soon after their people had suffered some kind of devastation (The Holocaust). *"Who hath heard such a thing? Who hath seen such a thing? Shall the earth be made to bring forth in one day? or shall a nation be born at once? for as soon as Zion travailed, she brought forth her children."* From this biblical prophecy and others, in conjunction with present world mayhem, we can understand why Christian preachers are convinced that the world is now in the midst of the end-time programme of events.

Global wars are breaking out as never before. In the last 100 years, earthquakes have increased tenfold. Famine in third world countries appears to be unsolvable as worldwide discord and rebellion escalates at an alarming rate. Crime is rampant. Divorce, abortion and drug abuse are on the increase and family breakdown is commonplace. The anything goes society, seemingly irreversible, is an integral part of western culture, with world stability a distant dream as governments continue to fail in their attempts to establish global harmony.

Once more, we can confidently refer to the Bible for answers, as a number of the end-time signs are clearly revealed in The New Testament.

End-Time Signs

- Matthew (24:7) states: *"For nation shall rise against nation, and kingdom against kingdom; and there shall be famines and pestilences and earthquakes in diverse places."*
- 11 Timothy (3:1) informs us explicitly: *"This know also, that in the last days perilous times shall come."*
- 11 Timothy (3:3) gives a clear account of the mindset of modern man, 2,000 years after it was written: *"Without natural affection, trucebreakers, false accusers, incontinent, fierce, despisers of those that are good."*
- 11 Timothy (3:4) adds: *"Traitors, heady, high minded, lovers of pleasure more than lovers of God."*
- 11 Timothy (3:2) gives us more: *"For men shall be lovers of their own selves, covetous, boasters, proud, blasphemers, disobedient to parents, unthankful, unholy."* No one could describe these perverse times more accurately.
- Matthew (24:12) tells of the hardness of man's heart in the world of today: *"And because iniquity shall abound, the love of many shall wax cold."*
- 11 Peter (3:3-4) says: *"Knowing this first, that there shall come in the last days scoffers, walking after their own lusts, and saying, where is the promise of his coming? For since the fathers fell asleep, all things continue as they were from the beginning of the creation."* The last sentence is an adequate description of the modern

day evolutionary view that the present is the way it has always been. God would have known that latter-day evolutionary speculation would be used by men as an excuse to deny His existence.

- 1 John (2:18) speaks of the many antichrist figures that have plagued the world during the last century: *"Little children, it is the last time; and as ye have heard that antichrist shall come, even now are there many antichrists; whereby we know it is the last time."* Hitler, Stalin, Pol Pot, Idi Amin, Sadam Hussein and others are antichrist type figures who are collectively responsible for the slaughter of many millions of innocent people, for no other reason but to satisfy their own Godless dictatorial ambitions.

- Luke (21:25) foretells of the many terrifying events that the world must endure prior to the second coming of Our Lord: *"And there shall be signs in the sun, and in the moon, and in the stars; and upon the earth distress of nations, with perplexity; the waves and the sea roaring."* To date we have not yet seen many unusual astronomical signs, but nations are blatantly in distress and the oceans of the world are certainly causing increased havoc around coastal areas in many countries.

- Luke (21:31) warns us: *"So like ye, when you see these things come to pass, know ye that the kingdom of God is nigh at hand."*

- Matthew (24:14) reads: *"And this gospel of the kingdom shall be preached in all the world for a witness unto all nations; and then shall the end come."* Despite what people say about the supposed decline in religious worship, the gospel message is spreading and reaching more people than ever before. Through television and the internet, the word of God and His Bible are being communicated worldwide, encompassing an increasing number of nations.

Matthew (24:3) explains how the disciples became anxious on hearing the end-time revelations: *"And as he sat upon the Mount of Olives, the disciples came unto him privately, saying, Tell us when shall these things be? And what shall be the sign of thy coming, and of the end of the world?"* Jesus replied: *"Take heed that no man deceive you. For many shall come in my name, saying, I am the Christ; and shall deceive many. And ye shall hear of wars and rumours of wars; see that ye not be troubled; for all these things must come to pass, but the end is not yet. All these are the beginning of sorrows."*

Regardless of our affluent western society, people are still facing a multitude of sorrows. False teachers, injected with satanic power are emerging throughout the world and as the Bible says, unsuspecting people are being deceived. Satan must be increasingly worried as the time of his demise draws closer. Revelation (12:12) informs us: *"Therefore rejoice ye heavens, and ye that dwell in them. Woe to the inhabitants of the earth and of the sea! For the devil is come down unto you, having great wrath, because he knoweth that he hath a short time."*

In the short term, this is not good news for populations on earth as it is evident from news rounds that world upheaval is escalating out of control. Despite the incessant optimism of world leaders, governments around the globe are floundering in their efforts to bring a lasting peace to their people. If, as it may appear, we are living in the end-times, then conflict and strife is destined to become much worse.

How bad can it become? I believe that we could be in the early stages of the worsening effect of world violence, catastrophes and turbulent living. While there has been a gradual increase in global mayhem for some decades, the frightening fact is, the graph is now beginning to turn sharply upwards. I believe that western standards of freedom, prosperity and opulence have reached a peak and henceforth, though it might still be some time away, the signs are that we are heading for a lasting decline.

At the time of writing, we are in the grip of the worst world recession for almost a century. Major financial institutions are going to the wall in unprecedented ways, as money markets seize up and banking giants tremble and crumble. Could this be part of biblical end-time prediction? There are many people who believe so.

We need to realise that these warnings were made some 2,000 and more years ago. Too many biblical signs are occurring to be coincidental and they are far too accurate to be ignored. The odds against biblical predictions being guesswork and taking place 2,000 years later are astronomical. By far the most significant of all end-time prophecies is the return of the Jews to their rightful homeland in 1948. God made a promise to His chosen people saying that He would return them to their homeland from the four corners of the earth, and He has kept that promise. During the 2,000 years of exile, the scattered Jewish race refused to fade away and die.

Satan is worried

God warns us through His Bible that Satan has been the hidden ruler of the earth since the fall of man. Does this not account for the wickedness and Evil that perpetrates mankind and explain why there is so much suffering for humanity to endure? When we observe the chaos and strife permeating all corners of the earth, there is no doubt that Satan has never had it so good. Those who are unaware of satanic influences in our lives do not possess the armoury to counter attack, virtually offering him a free hand in spreading his web of human misery. Just as Evil spirits cannot pervade our lives unless we allow them entry, Satan is unable to penetrate our defences as long as we adopt Godly ways.

Lack of devotion to God may explain why man finds it impossible to acquire a sustained happiness and peace of mind. While we are compelled to suffer the ravages of these latter days of Satan's rule, we can be assured that Christ has already embarked on a road to the recapture and restoration of His beloved creation.

Let us take a closer look at some of the end-time signs that I have mentioned above. World War One, at the time, was the most brutal and cruel conflict to face mankind in the whole of history. Having endured this savage conflict, the world had little time to recover when it was plunged into the even greater catastrophe of the Second World War, this time losing over 50 million of its inhabitants. Was this the prophetic teachings of Christ beginning to materialise?

Though world organisations pour trillions of pounds into fighting disease, their failures still haunt them. Epidemics suddenly break forth. Cancer continues to kill millions each year, in spite of the injection of astronomical amounts of money, and AIDS, pneumonia and many other diseases add to the toll.

Within families, which is the one environment where we should expect to find peace, harmony and love, there is a frightening and increasing trend of abuse, violence and disorder. Rebellious youths and disobedient children are, as never before, causing untold grief for their families and in their neighbourhoods, while discipline and the law are quite impotent in curbing these disturbing trends. The world's problems multiplying at an unprecedented rate is in perfect line with biblical warnings of the prophetic signs of the last days.

Countdown has Begun

We do not know with real accuracy the duration of these crucial years before the return of Christ, but the Bible has signified a starting point. The countdown began with the rebirth of the state of Israel in 1948, and many events since that time are in line with the biblical message.

In our emancipated world, the insatiable love of money and riches seem to rule people's lives. When wealth comes through the door, God is thrown out of the window. The Bible reveals that in the last days, men will be lovers of themselves and worshipers of money. These signs are evident, particularly among western societies. You may say, but surely man has always lusted for wealth. That may be true, but as I have previously mentioned, the graph is turning rapidly skywards and is symptomatic of prophetic end-time events.

While there is ample food to feed the entire world, there are still millions among third world nations who continue to starve. The Bible predicted that towards the end, world communication would be instant. This prediction has already come true. 24 hour news is with us through the medium of television. No sooner does a global event take place than we can know about it in seconds. We also have the internet and mobile phones which assist the process. No one in biblical times could have dreamed of such technology.

Over two thousand years before the car was invented, the Bible foretold that in the latter-days there would be chariots with lights travelling at high speed. Biblical man could not have envisaged such an invention as the automobile.

Signs of the end-times are occurring so frequently that it would seem foolish to ignore them. Jesus said that the time of the end would arrive like a thief in the night, when we are totally off guard: *"Watch therefore, for ye know neither the day nor the hour wherein the Son of man cometh"* Matthew (25:13).

Be prepared

No one but God the Father knows when Christ will be sent back to earth the second time. This is why Christ tells us to be ready and heed the prophetic warnings, so that we are able to understand and deal with them when they are suddenly thrust upon us.

The Bible speaks of the culmination of the end-times called the Rapture, when the righteous will arise from their graves and will be taken into the air with Christ. Next, the good people alive at the time will be taken up to join them. This will ensure that they avoid an earthly tribulation period of seven years, when the world will experience turbulent times unprecedented in history.

Prior to this tribulation period, the true antichrist will have emerged as a dynamic political figure, edified by other nations. He will deceive the world by his genius into thinking that he has the answer to world peace. The Bible warns us to beware of such a man and not to be hoodwinked by his charming but deceitful ways. However, many millions of the world's population will be fooled and swept along with his lure of peace and plenty.

Having become the most influential figure on earth and with nations under his spell, he will endeavour to control every human being on the planet. He will demand that every one of us take his mark to swear allegiance to him. Nevertheless, the Bible warns us emphatically that we must resist this mark at all costs. If we accept, there is no way back and contact with God will be removed forever.

Schemes are already in motion for the majority of nations to adopt ID cards in the next two or three years. It has been common practice for some time now for animals to be inserted with microchips under their skin, containing identifiable personal data, visible under scan. It is not unthinkable that people will be next. World organisations are already planning a cashless society and the natural progression would be the fitting of a scanning device under the skin, to be used instead of cash wherever we purchase our goods. With such a system in place, the antichrist would have a ready made worldwide snare to entrap his victims.

The good news is that the antichrist will only have his way for a time. The Bible tells us that halfway through the tribulation period (three and a half years), his plans to dominate the world will disintegrate. He will be exposed for the impostor that he is, and those who have succumbed to his demands will tremble at their fate.

There is no known, charismatic, antichrist type figure on the world stage at the moment, though it is said that he is alive and in waiting. We must be alert to world developments so that we can recognise end-time signs as they emerge. Satan, under the guise of the antichrist will plan to arrive on the world scene at short notice to catch as many people as possible off guard. Those who are unaware will be as lambs to the slaughter.

Believers at the time of the end will not have an easy ride. They will be ridiculed and belittled as 2 Peter (3:3) warns us: *"Knowing this first, that there shall come in the last days scoffers, walking after their own lusts."* In modern-day society, Christians are prone to suffer indignity at the hands of the ungodly, but this is an integral part of Christian living. As we draw closer to the climax of the last days, the ridicule and mockery will intensify.

You may question why we should worry or even think about such end-time events as they may not happen in our lifetime. This is the view of the Catholic Church. They do not preach end-time dogma. Their doctrine is to always dwell in the truth of the Holy Spirit and be prepared for the moment of death. As we can never be certain of future events, neither the time of our death nor the return of Christ, the Catholic Church prefer their followers to concentrate on the piety of their daily lives, abiding by the commandments as dutifully as possible and trusting in Jesus Christ as Saviour for their imperfections and failures. They believe in Heaven as their ultimate objective. With no prospect of Heaven, our short lives have little relevance and mankind is but a foolish creature without foundation or reason.

The Eternal Earth

The end-time does not mean the end of the world: *"Who laid the foundations of the earth, that it should not be removed forever"* Psalms (104:5). This confirms that the earth is never ending and was created for a purpose. 11 Peter (3:13) tells us: *"Nevertheless we, according to his promise, look for new heavens and a new earth, wherein dwelleth righteousness."* The change will mean a damaged world made good for man to inhabit in a lasting and satisfactory way. With Satan removed and unable to induce havoc into our lives, the Bible tells us that Jesus Christ will rule the new earth from His throne in Jerusalem. Where governments have failed, Christ will succeed. From the beginning, man has proven that he cannot rule himself successfully, and so we must rely on Our Saviour to bring nations together in lasting harmony. Jesus came to earth the first time to save us from damnation, so that after His second coming He could complete His mission and bring Divine stewardship to the whole earth.

How long now?

Can we measure the span of the last days? Christian Ministries have various opinions on the issue and this is the crux of the drawn out debate. Most preachers seem to be in agreement on the starting point of the end-times, which is the year 1948, when Israel was reborn. But when is the finishing point? Christian leaders and speakers are continually foraging for answers but the deliberation continues. The Bible does not give us a precise date for the end, only the signs. It appears that God may have done this to keep us on our toes, making it part of the great test of our faith.

Prophetic turbulent signs are on the increase and world catastrophic events are escalating. The insoluble question is how bad can these events become before the finale? Evaluating all relevant data, the extremes of speculation say that Christ could return to earth in the next decade or any time within the next 40 years. This leaves ample scope for the afflictions of man to deteriorate further and we must not get too carried away at this present time, lest we be hopelessly wrong.

The Bible states that from the rebirth of Israel, a generation would not pass away before the signs were fulfilled, but there are varied interpretations of a generation time scale. Some Christian scholars believe that a small percentage of the young generation living in 1948 would experience the end-time scenario. Since some people will undoubtedly live to be 100 years old, this could take us to the year 2048. 60 years have now passed since Israel's rebirth, leaving us with a possible 40 years to deliberate the final cataclysmic event.

While the world is experiencing much trauma, some countries continue to live in relative peace. There could be some time to go before the symptoms of the end spread to all nations on earth, and as the Bible tells us not to worry, it is our duty to continue in our daily worship until Christ decides the moment is right for His return.

Though we are forced to live under the ordeal of a fallen world, God has not made our lives unbearable. There is much to live for, and we should not allow end-time fears to tarnish our spirit.

Throughout the centuries, many people have attempted to foretell the date of the end, but all have failed with acute embarrassment, as predicted dates have come and gone with a non-event. How reliable is the Bible on this subject? Making one correct prediction 2,000 years into the future would be a great feat, yet amazingly the Bible has accomplished many. There is growing feeling and the evidence shows that the world is in the midst of some kind of critical countdown and many believe that the New York twin towers disaster was the beginning of that countdown. In recent times the world has faced the Indonesian tsunami, the New Orleans flood disaster, the China and Pakistan earthquakes and other calamities, where hundreds of thousands have died. If these events represent the early days of end-time turmoil, it is unthinkable what may lie ahead.

The Bible contains over 300 end-time prophecies of which many are taking shape before our very eyes. Some of the signs being observed today include the spreading of the gospel worldwide, false preachers, weapons of mass destruction, escalation of immorality, rejection of Godly truths, lawlessness, rebellion, the proliferation of humanism and essentially most of the ills of modern-day societies. It is true that some of these traits of man have pervaded for a long time, but many apply to the present day and would not be relevant for any other age.

It would seem incredible that all the biblical writers of end-time prophecies could be wrong. They are so accurate and in line with today's events that experts would deem it impossible for them to be in error. It is inconsistent to think that the Bible, having fulfilled nearly 80 percent of its total prophecies, could be wrong concerning these last days.

The global scene is changing at an unprecedented rate. During the last 40 years, the world population has rocketed from four billion to over six billion and it is estimated that man's knowledge is now doubling every two years. There is an uneasy feeling that humanity is heading for some frightening climax and that is exactly what biblical warnings are conveying to mankind.

High placed financiers and political groups are manipulating financial markets to bring them in line for a One World Government. The aim is to create a single world system, with one global government, a one world religion and one dominant financial institution, where every country and every citizen is centrally controlled. This system is in the making, is gaining momentum by stealth and may not be too far from fruition. The frightening aspect of the proposed world government is that it would be all set up and tailor made for the antichrist to step in, take control, and manipulate the populations of the world in order to execute his wicked manifesto.

During the latter half of the antichrist's reign, Evil of every kind will infiltrate world societies. Godly people will need to show inimitable strength of mind and fortitude, though it will not be impossible to survive and win through. The Bible tells us that the devil's reign will last only three and a half years and knowledge of this will assist us in our fight against him. During this period, faith in Jesus Christ will be paramount and those who embrace Him will have nothing to fear.

The Ultimate Victory

Finally, Christ will come and defeat Satan together with his followers in the final battle. Non-believers will be given one last chance to repent of their pagan ways and convey their trust in the God who offers them salvation. With Christ as our eventual ruler, world peace will dominate and the faithful can look forward to a lifestyle of lasting contentment. All the religious differences of humanity will come to a close as Genesis prevails over the Big Bang, the Cross vanquishes the Monkey and Heaven triumphs over Hades.

Whenever there is a major catastrophe, we will hear the ringing of the end-time bells. This is a natural reaction from end-time speakers. There will be other wars, major disasters and tsunamis, and human behaviour is likely to get worse rather than better. However, there will come a time when the pundits will be proved right. Christ has warned us that we cannot guess the moment of His return. We can only speculate. He has told us that He will arrive as a thief in the night when we least expect it: *"For the Lord himself shall descend from Heaven with a shout, with the voice of the archangel, and with the trump of God; and the dead in Christ shall rise first; Then we which are alive and remain shall be caught up together with them in the clouds, to meet the Lord in the air; and so shall we ever be with the Lord"* 1 Thessalonians (4:16 and 17).

As we emerge further into the 21st century, world recession is biting deep as global financial institutions flounder and governments falter. The planet which man has shamefully managed is running out of control and there is not a single person who knows how to handle it.

At the same time, Israel is at war, defending herself against the terrorists of Gaza, while fractions of world opinion turn against her. Could this be an integral part of biblical end-time prophecy, that prior to Christ's return, all nations will converge on Jerusalem?

Zechariah (14:2,3,4) states: *"For I will gather all nations against Jerusalem to battle; and the city shall be taken, and the houses rifled, and the women ravished; and half of the city shall go forth into captivity, and the residue of the people shall not be cut off from the city. Then shall the Lord go forth, and fight against those nations, as when he fought in the day of battle. And his feet shall stand in that day upon the Mount of Olives."*

Maybe the build up to anti-Zionism has begun, but perpetrators beware! Zechariah (12:3) gives adequate forewarning to the adversaries of God's appointed land: *"And in that day will I make Jerusalem a burdensome stone for all people; all that burden themselves with it shall be cut to pieces, though all the people of the earth be gathered together against it."*

Mingled with the sound of Terrorist/Israeli warfare, we may be attesting to end-time rumblings. The two are interlinked. As the wider world bears witness to current events in the Middle East and the increasing build up of animosity towards God's city, who can deny that the Return of our King may be almost upon us.

The important factor of the end-times is to be aware of what may transpire, so that if we are living to witness these events, we will know how to cope and be equipped to help the less informed, who will undoubtedly be perplexed and terrified by the mayhem that is unfolding around them.

CHAPTER SEVEN

A Life to Die For

The book of Genesis reveals how God's perfect creation became embroiled in sin, precipitating a gradual decline which has continued to this day. This degeneration of mankind during the last 6,000 years has resulted in wars, catastrophes, suffering and death. We know why men and nations continue to engage in hostilities and why there has never been a global peace since the fall of man. Informed Christians understand why we fail in our attempts to achieve ideal harmonious living conditions and why a loving God can appear to forsake us in our time of need. If we acknowledge biblical truth that the whole of humanity is vulnerable to satanic manipulation and sinful man is in tandem with him, we should not be surprised at the earthly turmoil that mankind must tolerate. Where Evil exists, Evil will infiltrate and we must never let our guard down against the tentacles of satanic power. In the final battle against Evil, Christ will rid the world of this contamination.

Biblical prophetic signs indicate that destructive satanic forces on this earth, while escalating, are coming to a close, and Jesus Christ is about to physically step in and restore His earthly creation to its initial perfection. The feeling that our world cannot continue to endure under the present turmoil, may turn to reality sooner rather than later. Signs denote that the present world system of things appears to be nearing a climax. Yes, I am talking about the end of the world, but not its total destruction. The end of the world in biblical terms suggests the end of our present system of living. A Third World War is the inevitable finale to these last days, but it will be short-lived, and thereafter a new, glorious and exalted existence will blossom forth for righteous people who have remained faithful to their Saviour. The refurbished earth will be their unending Heaven, having been renewed to the state of perfection that God intended in the beginning.

The Real Utopia

How will life be transformed in a divinely appointed earth? Would you like your new life to emerge without pain, suffering or disease? Could you contemplate living without any degree of stress and with no prospect of death to cloud your horizons? Can you envisage the world operating as one single state, with no disparity of race, without boundaries or barriers to hinder your movement and with no need for passports, visas or insurance? Supposing you could trust anyone you met and were able to forge instant friendships. Can you imagine an atmosphere where everyone loves everyone with no such human trait as envy, jealousy, hate, prejudice or discrimination? How about a world without currency and no bills to pay, where we could enjoy fulfilling, healthy, productive work, with amiable cooperation being the norm, as in one huge happy family. Would you be happy living in a situation where crime was non-existent, making the need for police, armed forces, security guards, courts and prisons, completely redundant?

Could you be satisfied living in conditions with no use for doctors, dentists or opticians and with no requirement for hospitals?

How about a life without sleep? Do you think that God needs sleep? I doubt it. Through His book of Revelation, God gives us the promise of a habitat without night or darkness, where we would never get exhausted, allowing us to relish the fruits of an unceasing consciousness under the guiding light of our Creator: *"And there shall be no night there; and they need no candle, neither light of the sun; for the Lord God giveth them light; and they shall reign for ever and ever"* (Revelation 22:5).

If we cannot trust our Creator to systemise the perfect environment, then where is our faith, and what is the reason for our confidence in God? It makes sense that God would wish to devise a paradisiacal setting for all the creatures on earth. It is rational to think that He would infuse our minds with positive emotions such as love, generosity, trust and hope, to the exclusion of hate, greed, anger and fear. If God can create a mighty universe encompassing everything within, including the inherent emotions of man, the task of affecting an earthly renewal within the realms of which I have described, will take little effort. Such a euphoric existence and more is not beyond reason in a world which God fashioned in the beginning and intends to re-establish at the end.

Can you recall how you feel on your best days and in your most blissful state of mind, when your feel-good factor is rampant and your achievements are accomplished? Ponder how you feel in those moments when love abounds, when your garden is trim and your house is in order and all is well in your earthly abode. Magnify those conditions a thousand fold, maybe a million, and we might touch on a scenario of what God has in store for His faithful.

Ecclesiastes (1:4) tells us: *"One generation passeth away, and another generation cometh; but the earth abideth forever."* We can be sure that this world is here to stay for an eternity of time, and the purpose can only be as a natural home for those who trust in God and wish to live under the direction of Jesus Christ as their Saviour and Ruler. Isaiah (45:13) speaks of the renewal of man: *"I have raised him up in righteousness, and I will direct all his ways; he shall build my city, and he shall let go my captives, not for price nor reward, saith the Lord of hosts."*

In His guide book, God leaves no doubt about His intentions for us in the new creation, but many, through their pride and vanity are in danger of exclusion from His covenants. Preferring to go their own way, they will use the gifts of intelligence and free will that God has bestowed on them to reject His offer of a timeless existence. 1 Corinthians (2:14) speaks of such people: *"But the natural man receiveth not the things of the Spirit of God; for they are foolishness unto him; neither can he know them, because they are spiritually discerned."* Proverbs (14:12) also emphasises this testimony: *"There is a way which seemeth right unto a man, but the end thereof are the ways of death."* The conceit and temperament of modern-man is a huge stumbling block to his vision of Godly truths.

One Final Chance

Knowing the affects of His scourge on creation and the satanic influence engaging men in wicked ways, God will give us every chance of repentance, especially at the hour of death. The Lord does not wish to lose a single soul, and those who have opted to lead unholy lives and die in the ignorance of their Maker, may for a few brief moments, as they pass through the curtain of death, be offered one final chance to choose the way of salvation or the road to damnation. Prior to and during the seconds of death the battle for possession of one's soul is intense, and God may disseminate His almighty power to enable unbelievers to evade the desperate clutches of the Evil One. This transient moment of death decision may well determine the direction of an eternal path. In His loving mercy, God may perhaps grant a sight of hell and allow some brief moments of precious time to choose the way to Satan or the road of repentance. Those who are familiar with the post death account of convert Ian McCormack, who having been pronounced dead by doctors, was granted a glimpse of Hades and subsequently returned to life, will bear credence to this possibility.

Many people have experienced similar phenomena. If God saved the soul of Ian because of a last ditch prayer of repentance, maybe He will afford the same opportunity to others. However, it would be presumptuous, a sin in itself, for anyone to lead an unholy life and rely on some last gasp deathbed repentance.

Unlike biblical times, God no longer speaks to us directly but He has not deserted us. Occasionally our lives may encounter His earthly presence under the most unusual circumstances, like the experience of a catholic priest who saw the face of Christ appear in the Host of the Mass, and the male nurse who witnessed a dark beam of light emerge from the head of a patient at the moment of death. I have personally experienced Divine intervention in the presence of a lady dying from cancer. In her fading moments, having received the last rites from a priest, she began to feel an outpouring of elation and wellbeing totally impossible in her physical state. That lady was Lena, my wife for 36 years.

The Earth Reborn

God has warned us many times against the sin of pride and its consequences, and how the opposing virtues of meekness and humility will reap the heavenly harvest. The Almighty does not break His promises and we can rely on His word: *"But the meek shall inherit the earth; and shall delight themselves in the abundance of peace"* (Psalms 37:11). There would be little benefit for inhabitants of the new earth if it were to remain in its present mode. The regenerated earth will enjoy an ideal climate, granting properties in the soil of the earth to be such that everything which blossoms forth will be disease free. Weeds will be a thing of the past and pestilences which can destroy crops and vegetation will become extinct. The range of natural foods available to us could proliferate enormously, with water and air consisting of the utmost purity.

The Bible informs us of a transformed earth: *"The wilderness and the solitary place shall be glad for them; and the desert shall rejoice, and blossom as the rose"* Isaiah (35:1). No barren land will linger in the renewed earth, where water will spring forth whenever it is required.

Isaiah (55:13) tells us that the unproductive things of earth will disappear and sprout anew: *"Instead of the thorn shall come up the fir tree, and instead of the brier shall come up the myrtle tree."*

Isaiah (55:1) explains how all of our needs will be at hand: *"Ho every one that thirsteth come ye to the waters, and he that hath no money; come ye to buy, and eat; ye come, buy wine and milk without money and without price."*

Several biblical passages assimilate the reality of the Garden of Eden which God originally planned for mankind. The meek who inherit the earth will have the ever enjoyable task of remodelling their earthly environment, to replicate the conditions which God intended before Adam sinned. Work will no longer be a chore. The innovation and creativity of man will blossom far in excess of his present accomplishments, with no deficiency of new horizons to explore.

Consider the technical achievements of the 20th century. After 6,000 years of progression, ingenious man has reached his present state of advancement by using a mere five percent of his brain power. Can you imagine the escalating scope of potential within us if we were to join forces with equally super intelligent people in a perfect environment for endless time? Perhaps it could transpire in a million years' time, when that potential has been fully consumed, that just as your computer may be given extra memory, God would simply add extra dimension to the mind of the new and elevated Homo sapiens. A fortunate few are born with photographic memories, who can instantly recall a wealth of data far out of the range of even the highest intellectuals. Imagine a world where everyone was endowed with the intellectual power to greatly surpass that level.

Though we may anticipate what life could be like in the Heaven on earth, we will fall short of the reality. Our earthly minds are finite, being unable to fathom God's perfect grandeur, as implied in 1 Corinthians (2:9): *"Neither has the eye seen nor the ear heard, nor has it entered into the heart of man what God has in store for those who love Him."* These assured words of God are intended to give us hope and strengthen our faith. If we do not believe them, then we do not believe God, and hence, if we fail to have faith in the words of our Creator, why should He take us to share His Heavenly abundance.

In the Good Book we are notified of the resurrection for all God's people. The good, the bad and the wicked will spring forth to face their eternal fate. Those who have passed the test of earthly apprenticeship will take up their position in the place God has prepared for them. The failures will meet their Nemesis. Possessions in our lives which we vehemently embrace will retain little prominence in the future world that God intends. Future possessions in our remodelled homeland are as yet an unknown quantity.

Eternal Youth

What price would we pay for a return to our youth? Despite the stress and heartache that life bestows on us, we would willingly tolerate a second life term if our youthful years could be relived anew. This is exactly what God has promised to those who choose to follow Him: *"His flesh shall be fresher than a child's; he shall return to the days of his youth"* (Job 33:25). Not only will we return to a youthful state, but our transition will remain immortal. God is no older today than He was a million years ago and those who reside with Him will exist in the same dimension. Our finite minds may struggle to grasp this conception, but it is logical to conceive that an omnipotent God, who had no beginning, will have no end. Earthly vision is restricted within the cordons of time, space and matter, while heavenly dimensions are timeless and limitless.

In the converted world, no one will harbour the inclination to disrupt a newly acquired peace. The "God is love" countenance shall be overwhelming. Unity and cooperation will so dominate the minds of men and women that any thought of antagonism or discord will become alien to one's thinking. The status quo shall rest on compatibility and unanimity, with our present earthly degrading attributes alien to our minds.

Not even a Sneeze

Our physical bodies, having reverted to a genetically perfect condition and congenial to an ideal environment, will grant us immunity to sickness and disease, even the common cold being a thing of the past. With zero demand for drugs and medicines, mind, body and spirit will operate with maximum efficiency and to a level which is unattainable in the polluted world of today.

Let us consider for a moment the millions of handicapped and disabled people throughout the ages who have endured their hardships, and perhaps wondered why they were afflicted with such stigmas. I believe that God has prepared a special place in His house for those less fortunate: *"The first shall be last and the last shall be first."* (Mark 10:31). Give a thought to their revelation in the new earth to come, when the blind will see, the deaf will hear and the dumb will speak. Reflect on the lowly gifted, now with super intelligence and the limbless with brand new bodies. Isaiah (35:5 and 6) makes this very clear: *"Then the eyes of the blind shall be opened, and the ears of the deaf shall be unstopped. Then shall the lame man leap as an hart, and the tongue of the dumb sing."*

In our renewed world, the Bible makes no mistake about God's intention to eliminate the bad apples. Wickedly influential people can contaminate society, cause wars, and turn neighbour against neighbour, with disastrous results. Proverbs (2:22) says: *"But the wicked shall be cut off from the earth, and the transgressors shall be rooted out of it."* There will be no place for troublemakers when Christ is Governor of mankind.

Reconstruction of this present earth will be total. All

creatures will become tame, as both animal and man revert back to vegetarianism, as they were in the beginning. Man will see an end to savagery in the wild and neither man nor beast will eat meat again. Cannibalism entered God's earth following the fall, and man was instructed to eat meat after the flood of Noah, when the creation of God descended into a new era of desecration which has continued downhill to this present day.

In our new earthly home, animal and man will combine to mould a fresh relationship as stated in Isaiah (11:6, 7 and 8): *"The wolf also shall dwell with the lamb, and the leopard shall lie down with the kid; and the calf and the young lion and the fatling together; and a little child shall lead them. And the cow and the bear shall feed; their young ones shall lie down together; and the lion shall eat straw like the ox. And the suckling child shall play on the hole of the asp, and the weaned child shall put his hand on the cockatrice den."*

Here, we are told that man and animal will live in complete accord and no longer be a threat to each other. We will play with tigers as we now play with kittens. We will be able to pat the crocodile on the nose without fear, and the birds of the air will land on our shoulders as all life reigns in a state of unison.

In the beginning, God formulated the character and instinct of animal and man to merge together with total cooperation, therefore reverting back to our original disposition with the animal world will assume a natural balance. In the regained relationship between man and beast, I believe that animals will be gifted a higher level of intelligence that they currently possess. This will strengthen the man to animal bond even more, placing communication at a more intimate level and forming an everlasting partnership of trust and respect, far removed from our present animal/human partnership.

Jesus Rules

With our new King in place on His throne in Jerusalem, the whole world will rest in the assurance of His governance for global peace and prosperity. Modern man cannot place his trust in governments to make the right decisions, but with one infallible ruler in Christ, we will be assured of a faultless system of administration: *"Of the increase of his government and peace there shall be no end, upon the throne of David, and upon his kingdom, to order it, and to establish it with judgement and with justice from henceforth even forever. The zeal of the Lord of hosts will perform this"* (Isaiah 9:7).

Weapons of war will be forgotten in the new Heaven on earth. Bombs, missiles, guns and tanks will be a thing of the past: *"He maketh wars to cease unto the end of the earth; he breaketh the bow and cutteth the spear in sunder; he burneth the chariot in the fire"* (Psalms 46:9). Wars which have ravaged our planet for millennia will cease forever as man settles into his new and blissful extravaganza.

Man will smile as never before, a deep, genuine smile, a loving and lasting smile. People will experience happiness, ecstasy and satisfaction on a level previously foreign to present human emotion. Modern man will fade as a forgotten shadow of the divinely enhanced individual that will become his ascendant. Remodelled man will be jubilant that his previously unseen God is now his earthly mentor whom he may see and meet in the flesh at a given notice.

Could you cherish an existence where death is extinct? Jesus Christ defeated death and passed that inheritance onto us: *"The last enemy that shall be destroyed is death"* (1 Corinthians 15:26). Earthly death is not the end, but the end of the beginning. Through dying on the cross and rising again, Christ reversed the process by which death entered the world. From this covenant of God, we need have no fear of death but see it as the passage to eternal life – A life to die for.

True Heaven

How does a new earthly Paradise and the highest Heaven reconcile itself with the destiny of man? While Christ rules on earth for a thousand years, as the Bible says, who goes to Heaven to dwell with the Father? I believe that a very special place, the true Heaven will be reserved for those who have loved and followed God faithfully in some intimate way. No one can be sure who holds or will earn this special favour. The Patriarchs, the Saints, the clergy, persecuted Christians and the devout people of God will all be in favour of the highest accolade, but only God knows who will have earned this highest reward. The Bible clearly exposes the difficulty of finding the Kingdom: *"Enter ye in at the strait gate; for wide is the gate, and broad is the way, that leadeth to destruction, and many there be which go in thereat. Because strait is the gate, and narrow is the way, which leadeth unto life, and few there be that find it"* (Matthew 7:13 and 14). These words indicate that a minority of God's people will make it to Heaven but that is no reason to be dismayed. Out of the billions of people born over the ages, the few in number will be a percentage of many. Everyone is presented with the opportunity.

Dare I suggest that the Heavenly paradise and earthly Eden may not be the only destinies awaiting mankind? *"In my house there are many mansions,"* says God. The universe is vast and who knows what other worlds God may have prepared for the countless people He has brought into existence. Who knows what further plans God had in mind when He created our earth in the beginning. If Adam had rejected Satan's proposal to eat of the forbidden fruit and man had progressed in the grace of God as intended, our present world would have adapted to a paragon of excellence and perfection.

What would the earth have been like if Adam had not fallen from grace? The descendants of Adam and Eve, living in a perfect earthly environment void of death and destruction, would have enabled the population of the globe to increase at an immeasurably faster rate than the past 6,000 years of man's earthly occupation. During the last 40 years alone, the population of the world has increased from four billion to over six billion. With no wars, disease or death to quell the growth, our original world would have filled to a comfortable level in a relatively short time, possibly a few hundred years. Knowing this, it is feasible that God could have prepared other worlds to accommodate His rapidly expanding family.

Would God have put limits on His planetary creations? I see no reason why. Maybe He created this enormous universe to give us a foresight of His intentions and the endless scope He has at His disposal. God is not governed by time, space and matter or the natural laws of science which He invented. Because His potential is limitless, we can only stand back in awe of what the future may hold for those who dwell in the Spirit and remain faithful to the promises of Jesus Christ.

The universe is vast enough for God to allocate every conceived person an expanse of their own, maybe to possess their very own planet, to be developed in accordance with the designs of their newly acquired superhuman capabilities. God must have had good reason to create the never ending universe. Just as we invite our friends to come and visit our homes, could it be possible to call on them to visit our uniquely designed planetary home in the reaches of space. Maybe Christ ascended physically up into Heaven from the Mount of Olives to demonstrate how we could also be transported through the reaches of space in the blink of an eye. We should never doubt what the Bible says, that with God all things are possible.

Could the gardeners of this world have the choice of owning their very own planet, awash with an endless array of magnificent gardenia for them to develop and enjoy on a level way beyond our present imagination? Maybe each individual will possess an accumulation of super talents to be developed in any wondrous way they wish.

We can be certain that the restrictions of our present lives, having evaporated, will open up so many options for us to explore our new found capabilities, that frustration and boredom will never enter our eternal activities. Heaven will go on and on expanding. Christ described Heaven as like the branches of a tree that diverge again and again in new directions, more trees and more options to continue without end.

If we could visualise and choose for ourselves an ideal existence with unlimited finances at our disposal, this would be woefully short of the plan which God prepared for each individual long ago. It is fun to contemplate the Hereafter, but the reality of a supernatural existence far exceeds the vision of earthly man. What we do know is in the written word of scripture. God's Bible, the embodiment of information, gives us an indication of our future make up, as in Philippians (3:21): *"Who shall change our vile body, that it may be fashioned like unto his glorious body, according to the working whereby he is able even to subdue all things unto himself."* Placing our trust in God to deliver and fulfil His promises will reap the celestial harvest. In order to achieve anything worthwhile during our earthly lifetime takes willpower and effort. To achieve eternal life is no different, as we focus our sights in a Godly direction and never look back.

The world is still reeling from Adam's sin and God cannot be happy with His broken creation. Jesus Christ is ready to come back and rebuild this shattered world, to end suffering forever and elevate man back to the position He initially intended for him: *"And God shall wipe away all tears from their eyes; and there shall be no more death, neither sorrow, nor crying, neither shall there be any more pain; for the former things are passed away"* (Revelation 21:4). This side of death's door may be fearful, but on the other side, the followers of Christ can anticipate an entire renewal. The former things (this present life) will be erased from memory as we become exalted to a pinnacle of enlightenment and infinite wisdom.

Only by the realisation that we live in a fallen and dysfunctional world caused by the transgressions of the whole of humanity, can we come to understand the significance of our topsy-turvy existence. Without this awareness, the meaning of life becomes a paradox and cannot be ascertained.

I prefer to think of our tumble-down earthly endurance and the 6,000 years of life on this planet as the teething problems of God's creation, after which we can expect a smooth and carefree ride into the depths of eternity. How long is eternity? If a bird were to fly down to a large sandy beach and remove one grain of sand every thousand years, by the time the beach was clear of sand, eternity would have just begun.